THE LAST OF
The Portadown News

Newton Emerson

Gill & Macmillan

Dedication

To my parents

Gill & Macmillan Ltd
Hume Avenue, Park West, Dublin 12
with associated companies throughout the world
www.gillmacmillan.ie

© Text, Newton Emerson 2006
ISBN-13: 978 07171 4103 6
ISBN-10: 0 7171 4103 9

Design by Graham Thew Design
Print origination by Carole Lynch
Printed by ColourBooks Ltd, Dublin

The paper used in this book comes from the wood pulp of managed forests.
For every tree felled, at least one tree is planted,
thereby renewing natural resources.

A CIP catalogue record for this book is available
from the British Library.

1 3 5 4 2

A Word from the Editor

It was hard not to be impressed by the towering new city centre headquarters of LENDU, the subsidised business agency.

'Do you really need a building this size?' I asked finance director Tessa Pepworthy, as a liveried Lithuanian maid set two cups of fairly-traded "Bean Counter" coffee on the teak boardroom table between us.

'Of course we do,' replied Tessa bluntly. 'LENDU couldn't function without tall storeys.'

The pleasantries dispensed with, it was time to get to the point.

'So why am I here?' I asked, assuming that the question would not be taken metaphysically.

'I think it's time you put out another book,' announced Tessa, dropping her voice to a conspiratorial whisper. 'The last one pumped an estimated £6,000 directly into the Portadown economy, so obviously we would match that with unsecured funding of £20 million, plus a free 5-year lease on an industrial warehouse and a ribbon-cutting ceremony by this year's secretary of state. What do you say?'

It was a reasonably generous offer, no doubt about it – but something told me to proceed with caution.

'I'm interested,' I said, after a sufficiently serious pause. 'But you're also my accountant, my solicitor, my agent, a major shareholder in a publishing company and the owner of Northern Ireland's largest chain of bookstores. Isn't there a potential conflict of interest?'

'Nonsense!' she laughed. 'I checked with our director of corporate ethics and he said the whole thing is completely above board.'

'Well of course he did, Tessa,' I sighed. 'He's your husband.'

'Now look here,' replied Tessa, furiously dunking a Rich Hob-Nob. 'We've been through this before. Northern Ireland is a very small place. That makes it inevitable that LENDU board members and leading figures in the local business community will know each other personally, or even be the same person, or possibly be different people with the same job. But that doesn't mean we're hopelessly corrupt. It just means we have to be rigorously accountable to ourselves.'

Tessa was right – we had been through this before, and it always ended with soggy biscuit on the teak boardroom table.

'LENDU is supposed to use its funding to generate wealth in Northern Ireland,' she continued. 'That means we can do either one of two things. We can give grants to multinational call-centre cowboys who are only marking time until Cambodia gets broadband – or we can pocket the money ourselves, bribe a planning officer, build an 8-bedroom mock-Georgian bungalow in North Down and prepare to sit out the next round of the Troubles in as much comfort as humanly possible. Now are you with me?'

'Tessa, Tessa,' I murmured, marvelling at her powers of persuasion. 'Did you ever think of going into politics?'

'Politics?' she replied. 'Jesus, Newton – forget about that bollocks.'

The Portadown News

6TH APRIL 2004   www.PortadownNews.com

Six more inquiries planned

by our security correspondent, Roger Base

IN A surprise move last night, Canadian judge Peter Cory has recommended a further six inquiries into suspicious deaths in Northern Ireland.

Jackie Fullerton's career
Blamed on old age despite perfect health. BBC cover-up suspected.

Shergar
Equine rights lawyer, last seen entering a Dundalk kebab shop.

Maysfield Leisure Centre
Killed during row over money. Belfast City Council accused of collusion.

Jane Kennedy
Disappeared April 2004. British Government may be responsible.

Jeffrey Donaldson's leadership bid
Definitely suicide, but David Burnside may have questions to answer.

1,854 IRA victims (and counting)
Securocrat-backed media conspiracy to undermine the peace process.

IMPORTANT NOTICE

This week we allowed a rich landowner to demolish an important WWII monument.

Please note that this still does not permit you to put up a garden shed or convert your loft without our permission.

BBC RADIO BLUSTER

Seamus Austin talks to DUP councillor Paul Dingleberry.

Followed by Sectarian Thought for the Day

Dingleberry: These inquiries are a concession to terrorists. What about the innocent victims?

Austin: You mean, like Robert Hamill?

Dingleberry: No! I mean Protestant victims.

Austin: You mean, like Billy Wright?

Dingleberry: Yes.

Austin: But wasn't he a terrorist?

Dingleberry: Look! You don't understand! THEM FENIANS GETS EVERYTHING!

...continued around in circles for the rest of our lives

PARAMILITARY FLAGS – MAN NOT ARRESTED

JUDGES HIT BACK

by our crime correspondent, Rob Berry

JUDGES have criticised Hugh Orde for accusing them of leniency.

"The Chief Constable is in contempt of court," said one judge yesterday.

"I sentence him to four hours of community service, suspended for two days, under the supervision of social services, acting on a care order, pending an appeal, in receipt of legal aid. Bail is set at 50p."

PORTADOWN NEWS INFOBOX

This week: How will students pay their tuition fees?

- Charging flatmate's girlfriend rent 23%
- Trusting in the power of prayer 1%
- Going back on the cider 48%
- Drug dealing 99%

OBESITY 'AGAINST GOD'S LAW'

by our health correspondent, Florence Vulture

GAY groups remain unrepentant for harassing Newtownabbey DUP councillor Arthur Templeton about his weight.

"Obesity is against God's law," said Northern Ireland Gay, Lesbian, Bisexual, Transsexual, Transgender, Transvestite and Translink spokesman Ben Dover yesterday. "The Holy scripture is quite clear in its disapproval of this disgusting perversion."

Biblical injunctions against corpulence include:
- Leviticus 7:23 "Ye shall eat no manner of fat"
- Isaiah 10:16 "Therefore shall the Lord send among his fat ones leanness"
- Deuteronomy 25:15 "Thou shalt have a perfect and just weight"

"I must remind Councillor Templeton that the body is a temple," added Mr Dover, "and not a Whitewell Metropolitan Tabernacle."

DE LERIOUS SPEAKS OUT

by our business correspondent, Reg Empty

CONTROVERSIAL businessman John De Lerious has finally spoken out about the collapse of his Belfast car firm.

"British secret agents destroyed the company," explained Mr De Lerious while wiping some coke off his nose with a £100 note. "Elements in the British government wanted the project to fail. While I never personally joined the De Lerious Motor Company I had some insight into its accounting…"

…continued in an eerily familiar vein for some time

Lawyer in terrorist associates shock

This bonfire rubbish is great!

King Rat would have loved it

The Portadown News

13TH APRIL 2004   www.PortadownNews.com

LE BON RECALLS RESCUE

by our sailing correspondent, Marina Carrick

DURAN DURAN lead singer Simon Le Bon has been re-united with the Ulster woman he rescued 17 years ago when her boat struck a reef off Venezuela.

"It was fairly routine," Mr Le Bon told our reporter yesterday. "Wherever you go in the world, there's always somebody from Northern Ireland getting wrecked."

What a load of rubbish!

As more and more residents complain about the bonfire rubbish blighting estates across Northern Ireland, the Portadown News presents this handy cut-out-and-burn guide to how those complaints are handled by the authorities.

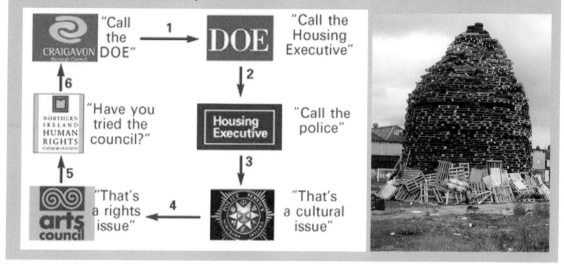

Culture Vultures

The Portadown News quizzes some young bonfire builders about their unionist heritage

Tyler Spide (15)

Q: Name three significant Protestant literary figures of the 20th century.

A: Wha'?

Grant Dole (16)

Q: What is the historical context of the Ulster-Scots musical 'On Eagles Wing'?

A: Wha'?

Glen Toran (9)

Q: Briefly outline Presbyterianism's philosophical contribution to the Enlightenment.
A: Wha'?

A doctor writes
The Portadown News medical column

AS A doctor I am often asked: "Where do pallets come from?"
The answer is quite simple. When a mummy pallet and a daddy pallet love each other very much they go out and get blocks, then bang them together while the mummy pallet shouts "Nail it baby! Nail it!" As they finish the daddy pallet screams "Take a load, baby! Take a load" and

Pallet-on-pallet action yesterday

CENSORED

Wake up to waste

(Unless it might involve taking on the loyalist underclass, in which case – just go back to sleep)

PORTADOWN'S FAVOURITE COLUMNISTS!

Judith Collins

Loyalists are dumping rubbish all over their estates. It's a disgrace – unlike wrecking the city centre, which was a regrettable but legitimate part of the conflict…

…and so on

Steven Queen

Dumping rubbish all over your estate is a regrettable but legitimate part of loyalist culture – unlike wrecking the city centre, which was a disgrace…

…and so on

An important health warning from Mackers

Bonfire smoke contains carbon monoxide, particulates and dioxins which can cause brian… brane… stupidity, like

Colombia 3 verdict due

by our Colombia 3 correspondent, Charlie Mortar

EL VERDICTO de la Colombia Tres es expected pronto. "Los Three Amigos es inocentes," said Sinn Fein humano rights spokesman Catriona Moustachio yesterdiá. "Es an blatant injusticia by PSNI muchachos y Branch Especial securocraté. Bastardos!"

El caso continua.

FAECAL ARBOREAL URSINE ALLEGATION

by our bear correspondent, Smokey Robinson

BEAR defecation is widespread in forested areas across Northern Ireland, claims the first report from the Independent Monitoring Commission, which reached its shocking conclusions after finding "lots of old newspaper and a very strong smell."

Those accused of dumping on the country include Adair Bear, Blair Bear, Bairbre de Bear and Grizzly Adams. Panda bears and Rupert bears were not questioned for security reasons.

"This society has reached a turning point," said IMC Chairman Lord Alderdice from his Balloo office yesterday. "Do we want to be care bears? Or do we want to be polarised bears? Now if you'll excuse me I have a cheque to cash."

A bear garden yesterday

On other pages

Unusual papal headgear suspected …p61
Blue tint found in upper atmosphere …p62
UDA arrests "out of the question" …p63

Belfast Tourism boost!

by our business correspondent, Reg Empty

BELFAST tourism is booming with an estimated 5.3 million visitors to the city last year, according to a survey conducted by people whose £80,000-a-year jobs depend on talking this up.

The massive influx of implied holidaymakers comprises:

- Shoppers – 2,600,000
- Commuters – 1,200,000
- People from Lisburn – 600,000
- Peace campaigners – 900,000
- Direct rule ministers – 50,000
- Arsonists – 12
- Actual tourists – 7

ULSTER-SCOTS AWAY-HAE

by our Ulster-Scots correspondent, Jock Dole

ULSTER-SCOTS Heid Yin Lord Laird has sensationally resigned in a row over funding.

"We are a unique people, proud of our independence and integrity," said his Lordship yesterday. "That's why we want a hand-out for our pretend language, just like the other lot."

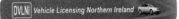

CUSTOMER NOTICE

Due to industrial action, you now have an excuse to stick it to the man by not buying a tax disk. Just remember that old cop trick about asking for your insurance certificate instead, knowing full well you have to send it off with your application. Good luck!

Yours in fraternal socialism

THE STRIKE COMMITTEE

Those new EU members in full

Cheque Republic
Likely to have a close working relationship with Dublin

Upper Anglo-Saxony
Pro-British, but too well-bred to make a fuss about it

Albania
Ancestral home of Alban McGuinness. Harmless.

Moronrovia
Many Moronrovians hope to study at the University of Ulster

Vulgaria
Large potential market for Claddagh ear-rings

Crime and punishment in Northern Ireland

Hot Property

with David Ervine

If you've recently had to pay a large fine you'll be particularly interested in a quick punt on the property market. Luxury city centre flats usually make a slow return but if there is an outbreak of mild intimidation in the area you could snap up a bargain, then make a juicy profit when the intimidation stops just as suddenly as it started.

Buy low, sell high as they say in the Pharmaceuticals Brigade. Good luck!

Bomb factory found

by our business correspondent, Reg Empty

INVEST-NI has welcomed the discovery of a bomb making factory in Strabane.

"This new facility will provide much-needed local employment for young people," said a spokesman.

"We were attracted to Northern Ireland by its low wages and excellent skill base," explained Real IRA managing director Ruari O'Bradaigh yesterday.

"The government also offered us an excellent incentive package."

The factory has now closed.

SINN FEIN WELCOMES NEW NIR TRAINS

It's a carriage of justice

Right, that does it. I'm calling the Pat Finucane Centre!

Bobby Tohill in court walk-out shock

Sod this - I'm off to the pub

PORTADOWN NEWS INFOBOX

This week: Why Catholics won't join the police

■ Fear of republican attack	67%
■ Fear of Nuala O'Loan	12%
■ Mum won't allow guns in the house	5%
■ Don't want to live in Moira	16%

The Portadown News

4TH MAY 2004 — www.PortadownNews.com

PROTESTANTS IN FLAT-OUT DENIAL

by our loyalist correspondent, Billy Shootspatrick

THE innocent people of Sandy Row are being terrorised by golf-ball throwing republican yuppies, claims Ulster Unionist councillor Nob Stroker. Residents marched on the upmarket Whitehall Square apartment complex this week demanding the immediate eviction of those responsible. "We are not anti-Catholic," said Councillor Stroker. "We are just anti-fenian."

Police monitoring the protest said they had no idea who was behind a threatening loyalist leaflet distributed earlier in the area.

"It could have been written by anyone," admitted PSNI officer Bill Mason, "where by 'anyone' I mean any one of the fifty loyalists behind me waving threatening placards."

The oppressed victims of Sandy Row yesterday.

IT'S NOT AN INJUSTICE

by our Colombian correspondent, Charlie Mortar

SINN FEIN has welcomed the acquittal of the Colombia Three. "The only thing anybody was guilty of in this case was undermining the peace process," said Catriona Ruane. "In fact, as far as we're concerned, that's the only thing anybody is **ever** guilty of."

ALLIANCE GO WITH GILLY

by our agriculture correspondent, Culchie McMucker

THE ALLIANCE Party has told supporters to vote for former Ulster Farmer's Union leader John Gilliland in next month's European election.
"Farmers and Alliance voters have a lot in common," explained a party spokesman yesterday. "We both drive Range Rovers, live off EU grants and churn out huge quantities of unwanted cheese."

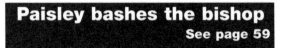

Paisley bashes the bishop
See page 59

Police forced to investigate murder

by our crime correspondent, Rob Berry

IN A shock move yesterday the police have agreed to investigate a murder.

Lengthy negotiations with the family of the late Mr Sean Brown have resulted in the following changes to standard PSNI procedures.

- Evidence will be collected
- Suspects will be questioned
- Arrests will be made
- Charges will be brought

If convicted, Mr Brown's killers will be sentenced to immediate release under the Good Friday Agreement.

BEL-TEL STRIKE

by our union correspondent, Jack Alwright

NEWS fans are bracing themselves for a current affairs shortage this week as Belfast Telegraph staff go on strike.

"I don't know what I'll do!" said one distraught local resident yesterday.

"Although I suppose I could just buy the Irish News and not read it until 3 o'clock."

Two wheels bad

by our peace process correspondent, Dale Sunning

THE North West 200 now kills more people than the IRA, according to a shock report from the Independent Monitoring Commission. Links to drugs, violence and Buckfast were also alleged, alongside an alarming increase in 'race hatred'. Organisers have reacted angrily to the claims.

"We have come to a fork in the road," said a spokesman yesterday.

"The British government must build straighter roads."

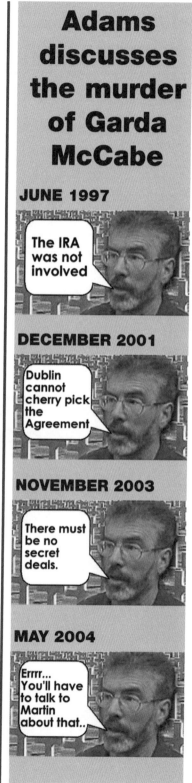

Adams discusses the murder of Garda McCabe

JUNE 1997

The IRA was not involved

DECEMBER 2001

Dublin cannot cherry pick the Agreement

NOVEMBER 2003

There must be no secret deals.

MAY 2004

Errrr... You'll have to talk to Martin about that..

PORTADOWN ABOLISHED!

THE planned re-organisation of local government will cost hundreds of jobs, officials have warned.

"I'll be out of work myself," said Portadown Council chief executive Tony Placement yesterday, "except for my other jobs at Portadown Regeneration, Portadown Together and Portadown Developments."

"I'll also be out of work," said Portadown Health Board chairperson Florence Vulture yesterday, "except for my other jobs at Portadown Health Trust, Portadown Health Action Group and Portadown Private Finance Initiatives."

"Even I'll be out of work," said Portadown councillor Marvin Currie, "except for my other jobs in Stormont and Strasbourg."

Due to redundancy payments, rates are expected to rise.

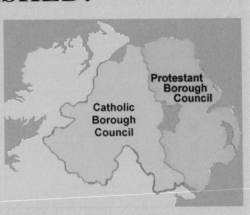

The proposed new councils

Protestant Borough Council

Catholic Borough Council

Balmoral Show Winners
EUROPEAN PRIZE CATEGORY

Billy Goat

High Horse

Poor Lamb

Belfast Telegraph reader searches in vain for mention of Belfast Telegraph strike

See page 59

CAPETOWN CRUSADER!

by our African correspondent, Cecil Rhodes-Service

SECRETARY of state Paul Murphy will travel to South Africa later this month on a fact finding mission.

"Northern Ireland has many lessons to learn from the success of South Africa's own peace process," explained Mr Murphy yesterday.

Those lessons include:

- Going back to majority rule
- Tolerating the world's highest crime rate
- Thinking that people like Robert Mugabe will just go away
- Claiming that tourism can solve everything

Tarzan of the Bungle

"I'm also hoping to visit the Orange Free State," said Mr Murphy, "and to learn more about Britain's role in the Bore War."

Tesco staff ordered off Glasgow plane

Pack your bags madam?

This week's cocaine seizures

Whiterocks

Coagh

Napoleon's Nose

PORTADOWN NEWS INFOBOX

This week: Why the Colombia 3 won't leave prison

- Miguel, Ernesto and Sanchez would miss them
- Can't find their passports
- Gives Catriona Ruane something to moan about
- Purer cocaine than Maghaberry

The Portadown News

COPS KEEP OFF THE GRASS

by our loyalist correspondent, Billy Shootspatrick

THE police are not withholding information on the UVF murders of David McIlwaine and Andrew Robb to protect an informer, insists PSNI officer Bill Mason.

"This crime has proved very difficult for us to solve," explained officer Mason yesterday, "despite a nightclub full of witnesses, hundreds of items of forensic evidence, a short list of obvious suspects, a local UVF leadership so cocky they were appearing on television at the time, and four years to figure it out."

However intelligence sources insist that the protection of informers is vital.

"Sure our guy stabbed two teenagers to death for kicks," admitted a spokesman yesterday. "But we have to keep him in place to stop something really terrible happening."

WEATHER

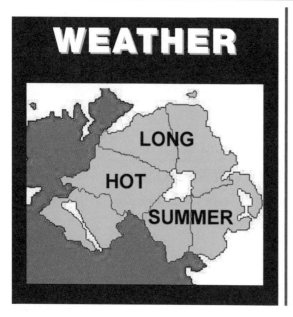

LONG HOT SUMMER

Nothing is sacred — official

MOTORMOUTH MAYHEM

**by our republican correspondent,
Anne Phoblacht**

SINN FEIN has criticised BBC presenter Jeremy Clarkson for ridiculing Bobby Sands over the dirty protest.

"Had the reference been made about a British soldier it would not have been broadcast," said party representative Raymond McCartney.

The BBC has accepted Sinn Fein's complaint.

"We wouldn't have made such a reference to a British soldier," admitted a spokesman yesterday.

"British soldiers don't smear shite all over themselves."

Free Presbyterians in "We'll convert priests" shock

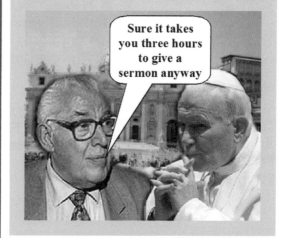

Sure it takes you three hours to give a sermon anyway

Alert on the line

**by our transport correspondent,
Fred Petrolhead**

THERE is a permanent alert on the Coleraine to Londonderry railway line.

"The line is closed due to a suspect package of measures," said Transport Minister John Spellar yesterday.

"A bus substitution service will operate forever."

LYRIC THEATRE

Some musical verse on the fire in Annalong Wood by Percy French (tune: same old)

Oh Gerry this London's a wonderful sight
You've people here worried by day and by night
They don't know to believe one damn word that you say
But they just keep on digging that hole anyway
Still for all that it matters we might as well be
Where the Mountains of Mourne burn down to the sea…

(chorus, repeat, repeat, repeat, fade)

A quick guide to justice in Northern Ireland

ILLEGAL   **NOT ILLEGAL**

PORTADOWN NEWS INFOBOX

This week: How can Northern Ireland lose weight?

- Point-scoring exercises
- Calorie Control Zones
- Couch potato famine
- Walking not talking

NEW! Eamonn McCann's Working Class Work-out

Sit-ups

Sit-downs

Socialist Environmental Alliance

The Belfast Telegraph

Press squats

Running Trots

Britain wants rid of radical cleric

Hilton Held Hostage

by our loyalist correspondent, Billy Shootspatrick

LVF MEMBERS evacuated to the Belfast Hilton due to the loyalist feud have wrecked their rooms, it emerged yesterday.

"This is a legitimate protest about conditions," said an LVF spokesman. "We will continue vandalising the mini-bars until our demands are met." Those demands include:

- Simply the Best rooms
- King Rat-sized double beds
- NIO suite-talking
- No wake up calls

"I'm afraid this is typical of the paramilitaries," said a security source yesterday. "They treat hotel like a prison."

Sinn Fein's paper tiger

by our republican correspondent,
Anne Phoblacht

SINN Fein has announced plans for a republican daily newspaper. The publication has the working title of 'Our Today Will Come' but sources say this is only provisional.

"We have to launch a completely new paper," explained a party spokesman yesterday. "Producing a Northern Ireland edition of An Phoblacht would be inherently partitionist."

ABOVE STANDARD BOG

by our conservation correspondent, Rusty Castle

WEST Belfast's Bog Meadows nature reserve has won a prestigious United Nations award for wild-fowl conservation.

"We hope this will reassure local visitors," said a spokesman yesterday.

"Every time someone says 'duck' around here they think Michael Stone is back."

Sinn Féin **An Ireland of Sequels**

Hang the bastards

Picture yourself as a **Lay Magistrate**

PORTADOWN NEWS INFOBOX
This week: What is the INLA feud all about
■ Drugs

TONY TACKLES TRIAD TERROR

by our Chinese correspondent, Paddy Rice

THE government has promised urgent action to address the threat of triad activity in Northern Ireland. Members of the Terracotta Army Council were flown to Downing Street yesterday where they raised a series of concerns.

Those concerns include:

- Cultural Revolution Rights
- Long marching
- Great peace walls
- The freedom to run a deadly criminal empire without fear of arrest or imprisonment

"We have agreed to all their demands," said secretary of state Mao Mowlam. "It's another Great Leap Forward for the peace process."

Holywood, ~~North Down~~ EAST BELFAST

Fashion victims group condemns paisley

See page 47

The Portadown News

7TH JUNE 2004   www.PortadownNews.com

Hospital hygiene horror

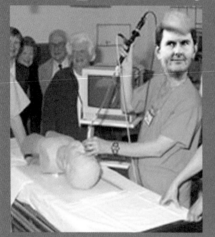

by our health correspondent, Florence Vulture

THOUSANDS of people in Lisburn have been sickened after having something rammed down their throats, it emerged yesterday.

Patients were unable to stomach the dirty Donaldscope due to contamination from previous operations.

"We should have sterilised it when we had the chance," admitted a Lisburn Hospital spokesman.

**Inside: Donaldscope Scandal –
PSNI applies for gagging order**

Out on his arse

by our policing correspondent, Roz Peeler

GAY-HATING Newtownabbey DUP man Arthur Templeton has been thrown out of his local District Policing Partnership. "Councillor Templeton's attitude was completely unacceptable," explained PSNI officer Bill Mason yesterday. "Everyone involved in policing must be prepared to bend over and take it."

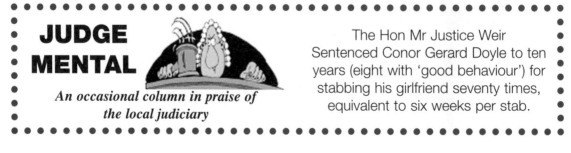

JUDGE MENTAL

An occasional column in praise of the local judiciary

The Hon Mr Justice Weir Sentenced Conor Gerard Doyle to ten years (eight with 'good behaviour') for stabbing his girlfriend seventy times, equivalent to six weeks per stab.

Community Forum

Shelley-Anne McAvoy explains why her son was throwing bricks on the Westlink

"OK, OK, so our Tyler's no angel but you've got to understand that there's nothing for kids to do around here – except for four leisure centres, two parks, eight youth clubs, three after-school clubs, twelve sports clubs, five football pitches, six libraries…

…and so on

Ervine enters smoking debate

I'm really more of a pipe man myself

Attempt to out-Shinner Shinners in out-Shinnered shock

DEMOCRACY FAILS AGAIN

by our peace process correspondent, Dale Sunning

THE vast majority of decent people in Northern Ireland are not decent at all, it has emerged.

Early tallies from the European election indicate that one quarter of the population are protestant bigots, another quarter are catholic bigots and the remaining half are too lazy to care.

"It looks like the fenians were right all along," said an Ulster Unionist Party spokesman yesterday. "Majority rule just doesn't work."

POOR TURNOUT BLAMED

by our republican correspondent, Anne Phoblacht

FIANNA Fail is blaming the poor turnout for its losses in the south's council elections.

"If Sinn Fein hadn't persuaded the poor to turn out, this would never have happened," said a spokesman yesterday.

PORTADOWN NEWS INFOBOX

This week: the Irish citizenship referendum

For the black babies

Against the black babies

Steven Queen

PORTADOWN'S FAVOURITE POLITICAL COLUMNIST

With the collapse of the SDLP and the UUP many people are asking: 'Is Northern Ireland heading for a two-party system'.

The answer is no.

Northern Ireland is heading for two one-party systems, which I'm afraid is something quite different entirely...

That's my comb!

The column where two bald men fight over a comb

DAVID BURNSIDE

Mr Trimble's possession of the comb has been a brush with disaster that can only lead to split ends...

...etc.

DAVID TRIMBLE

Regardless of Mr Burnside's interest in my scalp he must recognise the great job I've done with strand one...

...etc.

Where Eagles Derv

by our republican correspondent, Anne Phoblacht

SINN Fein's vital oil industry was crippled this week when Northern and Southern militias attacked the key Slab-Al-Murphy pipeline near the holy city of Armagh.

Sources say the attack was designed to undermine the provisional government, prior to the official hand-over of sovereignty which is expected any day now.

A crude device yesterday

"That'll be 30p a litre," said a republican spokesman yesterday. "Also, I can do you 100 Camels for a fiver."

Sick Parade

by our loyalist correspondent, Billy Shootspatrick

MATER INFIRMORU

TROUBLE flared at this year's 'Tour of the Ward' Orange parade after a gang of youths stormed into the Mater Hospital, threatening staff and patients.

"It was a misunderstanding," said a UDA spokesman yesterday. "They were just looking for Doctor Paisley."

Sinn Fein Pictures presents

INVASION

OF THE BODY POLITIC

NOW SHOWING
ALL OVER IRELAND

Lurgan Golf Club bomb - scores handicapped *See page 47*

The Portadown News

www.PortadownNews.com

PORTADOWN NEWS INFOBOX

How can hospital staff tackle loyalists?

1. Security operations
2. Superbugs
3. Drug replacement therapy
4. Brigadier-General anaesthetic

Rare Irish welcome for sick Polish migrant

Mmm... Nice arms

JUDGE MENTAL

An occasional column in praise of the local judiciary

The Hon Justice Shiel sentenced John Owen Conway to three years for a fatal assault, because he was drunk.
Verdict: Before you kill a man, murder a pint.

Violence passes off peacefully

by our loyalist correspondent, Billy Shootspatrick

POLICE have praised troublemakers for keeping Saturday's Whiterock Orange parade trouble-free.

"I was particularly pleased with the absence of paramilitary symbols due to the symbolic presence of paramilitaries, the recent lifting of threats due to threats from those recently lifted, and the general lack of violence due to the general violence of lackeys," said PSNI officer Bill Mason yesterday.

The Parades Commission has also thanked local people for respecting both its decisions.

Spot the UVF and win a Corsa

W5 DINOSAUR encounter
3 july - 3 october

Belfast City Councillor Jim Rodgers says

Bring *your* impressionable children to the Odyssey's council-funded dinosaur show, for an unforgettable anti-creationist experience!

Admission: There is no god

RESIDENTS WIDENED

by our republican correspondent, Anne Phoblacht

THE Roads Service has announced a resident widening scheme.

"Some women from the Lower Falls will not be fat enough to block the Westlink when it is upgraded from four to six lanes," explained a spokesman yesterday.

"We hope to rectify this by adding a lard shoulder."

PORTADOWN NEWS INFOBOX

This week: how Northern Ireland is changing

Ballymena deal 2003

Ballymena deal 2004

Spake Norn Iron

This week's word

GERRYPANDER

(Jerr:ee:paan:dur)

vb. Redrawing the boundaries of an agreement to benefit Sinn Fein

---

BBC RADIO BLUSTER

Seamus Austin talks to Orange Grand Wizard Robert Saulters.

Followed by Sectarian Thought for the Day

Saulters: The Portadown brethren will have to accept that they'll not be welcome in the Grand Lodge until they've engaged us in dialogue....errr....

ALL QUIET ON THE IRA FRONT

by our republican correspondent, Anne Phoblacht

BELFAST Deputy Mayor Joe O'Donnell has observed a rare minute of silence in honour of those who fell at the Battle of the Somme.

"As a Sinn Fein councillor, I have a great deal of respect for any Irish person who ever went over the top," explained Mr O'Donnell yesterday.

Good news for unsaved

by our business correspondent, Reg Empty

PORTADOWN home owners are celebrating the lowest Drumcree interest rates for a decade.

"I might actually be able to sell my house now," said Ballyoran resident Tessa O'Loan yesterday.

Drumcree Parish Church, Portadown, Co. Armagh, Northern Ireland

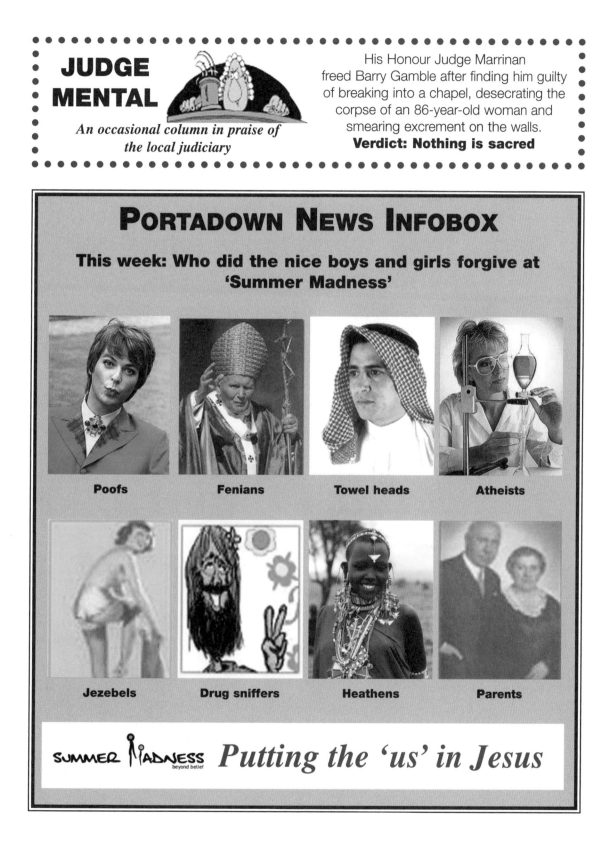

PORTADOWN NEWS INFOBOX

This week: Who did the nice boys and girls forgive at 'Summer Madness'

Poofs

Fenians

Towel heads

Atheists

Jezebels

Drug sniffers

Heathens

Parents

SUMMER MADNESS *beyond belief* — *Putting the 'us' in Jesus*

The Portadown News

5TH JULY 2004   www.PortadownNews.com

Teen Satanists on drugs steal Viagra from sweetshops while gay councillors mock Jesus

by our circulation correspondent, Jason Lowbrow

On other pages:

- Belfast Telegraph sales fall
- News Letter sales fall
- Scraping sound heard from barrel

Speaker's Corner

This week: Republican Sinn Fein's Ruari O'Bradaigh explains how sending letter bombs will bring about a united socialist Ireland

"The so-called 'Royal Mail' is a monarchist institution – indeed it is synonymous with the original 'Royal Male', King William of Orange. Or should that be homonymous? In either case we will stamp it out with a package of measures that will push the envelope of republicanism and deliver first-class Irish freedom.

The queen may think we need her to get sorted, but as I mentioned in a previous address, we'll soon have her licked and then we'll have seen the back of her..."   **...and so on**

National Stadium sites 'all unsuitable'

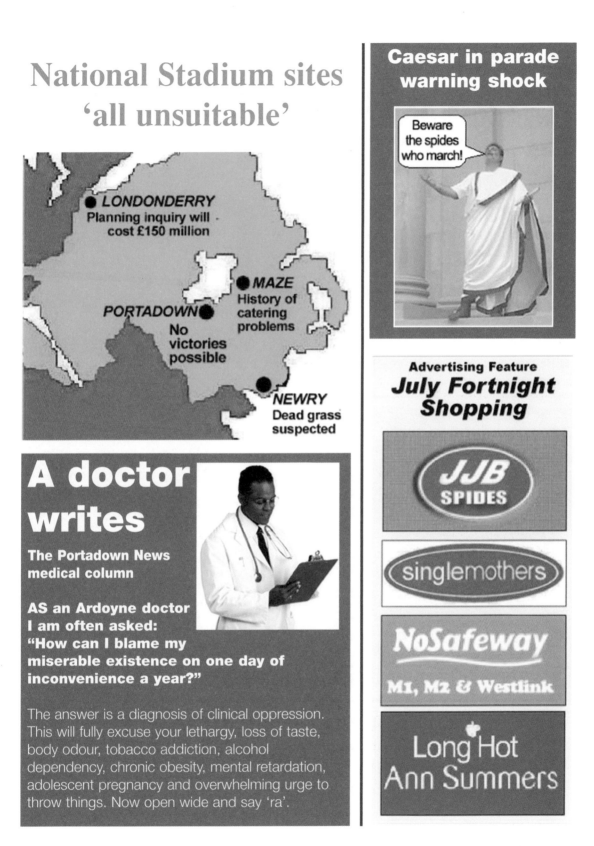

LONDONDERRY
Planning inquiry will cost £150 million

MAZE
History of catering problems

PORTADOWN
No victories possible

NEWRY
Dead grass suspected

Caesar in parade warning shock

Beware the spides who march!

A doctor writes

The Portadown News medical column

AS an Ardoyne doctor I am often asked: "How can I blame my miserable existence on one day of inconvenience a year?"

The answer is a diagnosis of clinical oppression. This will fully excuse your lethargy, loss of taste, body odour, tobacco addiction, alcohol dependency, chronic obesity, mental retardation, adolescent pregnancy and overwhelming urge to throw things. Now open wide and say 'ra'.

IT'S AN ORANGE SELL-OUT!

by our retail correspondent, Kaye Mart

HUGE crowds have flocked to Antrim to celebrate the 12th of July in true Protestant fashion.

"These Junction One bargains have saved us a fortune on sectarian labels," said one loyal customer yesterday as he marched straight to the check-out.

"Now I just hope some twat hasn't blocked the M2 or we'll never get home in time for Coronation Street."

On other pages:

■ Belfast scum tear lumps off each other – no shoppers injured

All prices sashed!

MEMOIR MENTION

by our American correspondent, Brad Cheeseburger

A local girl has been mentioned in Bill Clinton's memoirs.

"I will always remember the touching letter I received from Shelley-Anne McAvoy, aged 17, from the Irish and Northern Irish town of Portadown," writes the former president on page 934.

"'Dear Mr Clinton', she wrote, 'Why is your card shop in the High Street Mall so shite? Nobody wants Take That calendars any more and Purple Ronnie is just stupid. Love, Shelley-Anne'."

PORTADOWN NEWS INFOBOX
This week: how the peace process works

1. Gardai accused of corruption for claiming to know where IRA weapons are buried
2. Gardai not accused of corruption for claiming not to know where IRA weapons are buried

Arm decommissioned

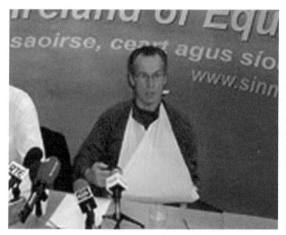

by our republican correspondent,
Anne Phoblacht

ONE of the IRA's deadliest arms has been surrendered.

Gerry Kelly's broken limb was presented to the media this week after Sinn Fein medical staff had carefully cast the blame.

"Fortunately the wrist and elbow are undamaged," said a party spokesman yesterday. "As you know, Gerry is particularly fond of his joints."

It is believed that Mr Kelly is coping well without his arm, having spent much of his life completely legless. However security sources indicate that several teenage girls have yet to be debriefed due to the incident.

Confused Christian pickets UTV over embryo screening

See page 47

Holiday weather

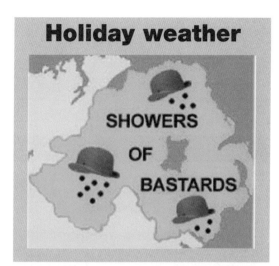

Spake Norn Iron

This week's word

SANCTIMONEY

(sank:tuh:mun:ee)

n. Financial assistance to the Andersonstown News

DUP considers compromise

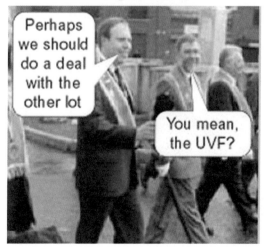

The Portadown News

26TH JULY 2004　　　www.PortadownNews.com

LITERALLY RIDICULOUS

by our security correspondent, Roger Base

SECURITY chiefs have been criticised following the disappearance of a document from Castlereagh.

The document is believed to contain the names of people suspected of stealing documents.

"This is a clear case of recursive self-referencing," explained Craigavon University semiotics professor Noel Champsky yesterday. "The security forces must take a more deconstructive attitude."

In an epistemologically relative statement, security minister Ian Pearson said "This is not a statement."

Down the back of a radiator yesterday

Bonfire of the Inanities

PORTADOWN NEWS INFOBOX

This week: The new domestic rating system

To ensure fairness, from 2006 household rates in Northern Ireland will be calculated using the following simple formula:

$$\oint B \cdot ds = \mu_0 \int J \cdot dA + \mu_0 \varepsilon_0 \frac{d}{dt} \int E \cdot dA$$

$$\oint E \cdot ds = -\frac{d}{dt} \int B \cdot dA$$

$$\oint B \cdot dA = 0$$

X = Distance from Lurgan
Y = Number of conservatories
Z = Volume of wheelie bin
A = Acres of laminate flooring
B = Decking/patio ratio
C = Height of bad taste

RHUBARB, NO CUSTODY

by our crime correspondent, Rob Berry

THE PSNI has appealed to local people to help prevent racist petrol bomb attacks.

"Everyone in the community knows who is carrying out these attacks, except me," said community police officer Bill Mason yesterday. "Without the assistance of the community we can't help the community to rid itself of those elements within the community who are targeting members of the ethnic community within the community. I appeal to anyone in the community with information to inform us, unless their information involves an informer."

"It is only a matter of time before an entire family is burnt alive," added officer Mason. "Fortunately, that's the fire brigade's problem."

Have Your Say!

Should the Londonderry railway line be closed?

Eamonn McCann, Derry

"First class, yes. Working class, no."

Martin McGuinness, Bogside

"Close the line? Is this some kind of hoax?"

John Hume, Foyle

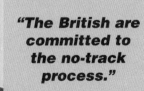

"The British are committed to the no-track process."

Jeffrey Donaldson Lagan Valley

"But I've already changed at Lisburn!"

Cops in yellow peril

by our security correspondent, Roger Base

Another black day for white people yesterday

LOYALISTS have advised ethnic minorities in South Belfast that more police warnings are imminent.

"Obviously an informer tipped the cops off about this weekend's attacks," said community representative Billy Shootspatrick. "So now we have to plan more attacks to find out who squealed."

"We have received information that more attacks are planned," confirmed PSNI officer Bill Mason several minutes later. "But I'm afraid I can't be more specific, as that would compromise our informer."

Spake Norn Iron

This week's word

ALEXICON

(aah:leks:ee:kon)

n. List of big words the Sinn Fein press office has taught Alex Maskey

---

PORTADOWN NEWS INFOBOX

This week: Why a former NI Secretary of State will make a great European Commissioner

- Knows the British can't be trusted
- Likes giving the Irish money
- Familiar with useless parliaments
- Believes in unwieldy unions
- Happy lecturing people about democracy while holding an unelected office

'Isle be back' - Adams

by our republican correspondent, Anne Phoblacht

GARDAI have discovered a large republican arms dump on a small island.

"This is a fairly remote location, lying just west of Scotland in the Atlantic," explained garda Bill O'Mason yesterday.

"We can't say how long the weapons have been there as we have never searched this particular island before."

Notice of planned strike

DEMOLITION OF GRADE TWO LISTED CIVIL SERVANTS AND REPLACEMENT WITH FLYING PICKET FENCE AND DEADLINE EXTENSION. ALSO REMOVAL OF TREES.

SQUEEZE-BOX SAVED

by our health correspondent, Florence Vulture

CRAIGAVON Hospital's depression chamber has been saved from closure.

Use of the chamber has risen over the past few years due to the popularity of nosediving. "This facility is essential to Northern Ireland," said health spokesman Angela Crippen. "We need to put pressure on almost everyone who surfaces around here."

The Portadown News

9TH AUGUST 2004   www.PortadownNews.com

HIPPOCRATIC OAF

by our health correspondent, Florence Vulture

ONLY real doctors were allowed to treat Dr Ian Paisley during his stay in hospital this week, it has emerged.

"The soul is eternal while the body is but a fleeting vessel," confirmed a DUP source yesterday.

"That's why you can't trust your body to some bloke with a $50 mail-order certificate from Kentucky."

Dr Paisley's real doctors gave him the all-clear after a routine bile transfusion.

"The operation was an unqualified success," said a hospital spokesman. "Much like Dr Paisley himself."

ENVOY IN COY PLOY

by our American correspondent, Brad Cheeseburger

AMERICAN special envoy Mitchell Reiss has finally explained how his comments about the Orange Order were taken 'out of context'.

"My e-mail was written in the context of thinking the Irish News wouldn't get hold of it," said Mr Reiss yesterday.

That e-mail in full:

Themmuns

File   Edit   View   Insert   Format   Tools   Message   Help

From: Mitchell Reiss, US Special Envoy
To: Father Sean McAnus, Irish-American Unity Conference
Cc: Nobody, especially the Irish News
Subject: Themmuns

Dear Father McAnus

I hate those orange bastards.
They're a bunch of c***s.

Yours
Mitchell

Asbestos Crumlins
a great fibre provider

Apprentice Boys parade 'definitely not gay'

See page 42

Spake Norn Iron

This week's word

CAHILLWALKING

(Kah:hil:wawk:ing)

v.n. Goose-stepping behind the coffin at an IRA funeral. see also: Eva de Bruin

They'll have to go away you know

BENT COPPER CRISIS

by our lifestyle correspondent, Ben Dover

THERE has been heavy criticism of the police presence at this year's Belfast gay pride parade.

"My God, those new uniforms are just awful," said a parade spokesman yesterday.

"I'm all for the full implementation of Patten, but did they have to get rid of the helmets, the truncheons, the rubber bullets?" *...and so on*

SHELLEY-ANNE FOYLED AGAIN

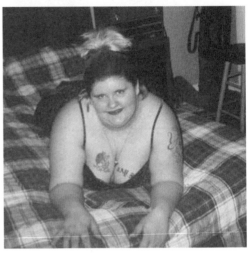

by our North West correspondent, Dermot Londondermot

APPRENTICE Boy Billy Shootspatrick (28) finally became a man last night with the help of local maiden Shelley-Anne McAvoy and three bottles of Buckfast.

"I'm no Lundy, but I left the gates wide open," the popular 17-year-old told reporters this morning.

"The wine was fortified yet I was defenceless."

However Shelley-Anne says that Billy still has much to learn.

"I'm besieged by men all the time, so I'd like to offer Billy some advice," she said. "Next time you storm the ramparts, don't go straight for The Diamond."

Who will replace Dr Ian Paisley?

Peter Robinson
Hardline second in command willing to compromise

Nigel Dodds
More willing to compromise than second in command

Jeffrey Donaldson
Will compromise hard for a second command

Ian Paisley Junior
Second in line but hardly commanding

Sammy Wilson
Compromised but will go hard on command

Reverend Willie McCrea
Fuckwit

Pull the udder one

by our agriculture correspondent, Culchie McMucker

SOUTH Armagh group Farmers Who Are Obviously Provos say army surveillance equipment is responsible for the recent birth of a two-headed calf.

"The fact that all my fields are saturated with red diesel has nothing to do with it," explained FWAOP spokesman Josias Bogman yesterday.

"I demand compensation and in fact I demand double compensation, as technically I am claiming for two head of cattle."

Bush forms concerned presidents committee

See page 47

The Portadown News

30TH AUGUST 2004   www.PortadownNews.com

Depression strikes Derry

by our North West correspondent, Dermot Londondermot

THERE were scenes of devastation in Derry this week after hundreds of people suffered a misfortune for which nobody else could be blamed.

Damage was worse in the Dunkcastle, Notshallow and Stranded Road areas, where raw sewage poured into a bar that normally only smells of piss. A large number of the city's famous whine cellars were also destroyed.

"The government, the water service, the fire brigade, the insurance companies - they're all completely useless," said one local resident yesterday. "Realistically, I can't pin this on any of them."

"All the water fell on this side while none fell on the Waterside," complained another. "It's blatant precipitation."

In other news: Blame in Spain falls mainly on the rain

Spake Norn Iron

This week's word

DUPlicity

(Joo:pliss:ah:tee)

n. Claiming you aren't prepared to do a deal as preparation for the deal you are about to do

---

INSECTARIAN ATTACK

by our security correspondent, Roger Base

PEST control experts battling the mid-Ulster wasp infestation have called in the Bee Specials. "We'll be smoking them out with a sting operation - possibly a honey trap," said PSNI officer Bill Mason yesterday. "Their precious queen won't save them now."

A White Anglo-Saxon Protestant yesterday

Stop these cocks!

by our crime correspondent, Rob Berry

An illegal pipe band yesterday

SECRETARY of state Paul Murphy is planning unnecessary rate rises before water privatisation to make the new bills seem reasonable, it has emerged.

"This is entirely normal Northern Ireland Office procedure," explained an NIO official yesterday. "For example, we let republicans kill people before the ceasefires to make Sinn Fein seem reasonable, we let loyalists kill people before the Agreement to make the peace process seem reasonable and we let Gerry Adams kill the Ulster Unionists before the last election to make the DUP seem reasonable. Now piss off."

Bigot accused of being estate agent

See page 42

Joe O'Donnell Developments
(A division of Murphy's Slabs)

The Safehouse
Deceptively specious

The Flat-Denial
For those who prefer tall storeys

The Terrorace
Speciously deceptive

Subject to planning permission
Gardens optional

Oh for God's sake hurry up and die already

by our health correspondent, Florence Vulture

IAN Paisley has threatened to sue newspapers following speculation over the state of his health.

"These lies are the work of Romanist journalists, my doctors and anyone with eyes in their head," croaked the DUP leader.

"I will still be flying to the talks in England this month to make sure that my party colleagues don't talk to anybody."

The DUP confirmed Dr Paisley's imminent departure and advised supporters to gather at Aldergrove Airport.

"The situation is grave," said a spokesman yesterday.

"Peter Robinson will make a terminal statement once we've dropped off our baggage."

JUDITH COLLINS

The column that holds nothing up

Ten years since my new friends stopped killing Protestants, it is important to remember that the real enemy was the British. All those dead Protestants were just stupid collaborators who got in the way.

Once the surviving Protestants understand this they will happily support a united Ireland!

Next week: Playing to the gallery – the new playing with yourself?

The Phone Book Experiment

Can I have the old phone book back?

No

Hydraulic ram raid

by our North Belfast correspondent, N. Claves

Another Hole in the Wall Gang atrocity

TENSIONS are at breaking point in North Belfast after this week's attack on a bar, warn community representatives.

"Loyalism has come to a fork lift in the road," said Sinn Fein councillor Anne Phoblacht. "They can not cherry-picker the Agreement."

Disband?

No, dat band

More bullets lost in post

See page 42

The Portadown News

6TH SEPTEMBER 2004 www.PortadownNews.com

NEW HOPE FOR TRAGIC COUPLE

by our fertility correspondent, Urethra Franklin

A LOCAL couple have been given the go-ahead to conceive something embryonic.

Their existing children suffer from a bad-blood disorder which can only be cured by discarding a lot of useless abortions.

Medical experts say the procedure will not hurt at all but a great deal of screaming is still expected, particularly when the umbilical is cut.

"This does raise a number of ethical concerns," admitted practising obstinatrician Dr Gerry Adams yesterday, "but then that's never stopped me before. The main thing is not to think of what we've killed as human, and to remember that it all stems from the cells."

Yanks walk the plank

by our American correspondent, Brad Cheeseburger

THOUSANDS of American cruise ship passengers have arrived in Belfast on board the liner Enormous Princess.

"We just love it here," said Kristal Heffelump from Pullover, New Jersey.

"It's nice to find somewhere in Europe where we don't seem particularly fat."

The Last Supper

Argentine president Lula da Silva in David Jones shock

Spotter: John McCann

GAELS MAKE THEIR PITCH

by our sports correspondent, A. Bore

The GAA has agreed to support Northern Ireland's new national stadium, subject to several conditions.

"We want a level playing field, seats in both stands and no rugby union," said a GAA spokesman yesterday.

"Also, any grass will be shot."

Holiday 'ruined' by total destruction of Caribbean

See page 42

Reserve price met

by our policing correspondent, Roz Peeler

The owners of a small Scottish pub which went on the market last Thursday say they are mystified by the level of interest from Northern Ireland.

"We've had 820 offers, all for the asking price of £100,000, from gentlemen with Ulster accents," said landlord Jock Drambuie yesterday.

Joe O'Donnell Developments

(A division of Murphy's Slabs)

is proud to present:

Dunkillin Dunes

Donegal retreats for just £300/week

Catriona says Bring Him Home!

Conflict resolution expert and non-Sinn Fein member Mark Thatcher is being denied his hooman rights in a foreign jail because of his opposition to a brutal regime!

BBC RADIO BLUSTER

Seamus Austin goes live to our reporter Jack Shortstraw at the gates of Leeds Castle.

Followed by Sectarian Thought for the Day

Seamus: So what's going on in there Jack?

Jack: A mile behind me in the loveliest castle in the world, home to kings and queens down the ages, encircled by a swan-filled moat, protected by sturdy battlements whose ancient stones have witnessed a thousand years of British history, I have no more idea than you do.

Talks end in more talk

by our peace process correspondent, Dale Sunning

THE LEEDS CASTLE peace talks have ended in failure with both sides agreeing they were not a failure.

Sinn Fein has agreed to disband the IRA but failed to agree on how to operate the assembly when it refuses to disband the IRA.

The DUP has agreed to share power with republicans but failed to agree on how to operate the assembly when it refuses to share power with republicans.

The British government has ruled out further all party talks to encourage all parties to keep talking.

"This is the last time we're doing this," Tony Blair told reporters yesterday. "See you next time."

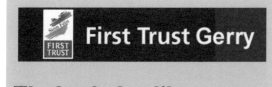

First Trust Gerry

The bank that likes to say:

'Empty this cash machine or we'll kill your family'

Malachi O'Doherty in Patrick Magee shock

Stormont Castle
'The unloveliest castle in the world'
Ideal for:
- Shotgun weddings
- Forced retirements
- Tactical weekend retreats

The Portadown News

20TH SEPTEMBER 2004   www.PortadownNews.com

Bug discovered up Sinn Fein's arse

by our security correspondent, Roger Base

SINN FEIN has found another bug up its arse.

Republicans claim the device is of British origin and has been bugging them for years.

Security sources say they are not surprised by the revelation.

"Sinn Fein always has a bug up its arse over something," said an expert yesterday.

FRUIT OF THE LOOM®
Spinning LEDU a yarn since 1987

- **Paul Murphy collapses**
- **Blair in heart scare**
- **Paisley still not dead**

Politics quits Morgan

by our republican correspondent, Anne Phoblacht

Politics has announced that it is quitting Martin Morgan.

"I feel that I have gone as far as I can go with Martin Morgan," said politics yesterday.

"The time has come for me to move on and concentrate on the people who matter to me."

GERRY TO THE RESCUE!

by our Middle East correspondent, June Sands

GERRY ADAMS has broadcast a personal appeal to the kidnappers of British hostage Ken Bigley.

"Keeping this man in a cage and threatening to cut off his head is no way to advance your cause," Mr Adams told Arabic Ulster-Scots TV channel Al-Dya'seeher yesterday.

"Instead, Mr Bigley should be taken to a remote barn, strung up by the arms, tortured and savagely beaten for several weeks, interrogated at gunpoint, sentenced to death by Danny Morrison, shot once through the back of the head, dumped in a bog somewhere and never mentioned again."

"You could also use him as a proxy suicide bomber," added Mr Adams. "I've been in touch with his family, so I have their address if you need to kidnap them as well."

Sharp rise in repossessions

Senior Citizen Travel-Pass
This card entitles the holder to free cross-border travel

Name:
Ian Paisley
Age:
78

Baile Atha Cliath

Michelle Gildernew in Mary Harney shock

'MIGHT, NOT, BYE'

An exclusive extract from the authorised biography of Jeffrey Donaldson, aged 5'2"

Ken Magennis was on his knees, but he was no Jim Molyneaux. "Look, Ken," said Jeffrey, staring him straight in the eye, "My conscience is more important to me that party unity, yet not important enough to leave before splitting the party. Goodbye!"

"No! No!" cried Magennis. "This is unconscionable!"

"How will history judge me now?" wondered Donaldson, as he rode his Shetland pony out through the gates of Cunningham House. "What price my conscience?"*

£9.99 for a short while, then £1.50 at Booksavers

Department of Health, Social Services and Public Safety

NEW ABORTION GUIDELINES

EasyJet: 0870 600 0000

SeaCat: 08705 523 523

BBC RADIO BLUSTER

Seamus Austin talks to prospective Westminster candidate Mrs Daphne Trimble

Followed by Sectarian Thought for the Day

Seamus: Won't the DUP beat you?

Daphne: That never stopped Iris Robinson.

'From Fags to Riches'

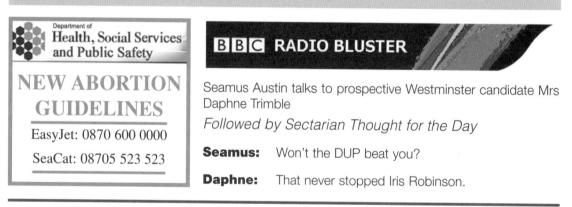

CATEGORY: HISTORICAL ROMANCE

PUBLISHER: MILLS & BOMB

"Smoking indeed! I will not hear of such a thing and neither will maiden aunt Bairbre," said Lady Mary Lou, her pert young breasts heaving like two ripe Brussels sprouts.

"Then you have spurned my estate and forfeited your inheritance," said Lord Gerry, angrily ringing the butler's bell. "Martin!" he cried. "Lock that coachman in the dungeons and bring me another 6,000 boxes of tobacco!"

Stoops to conquer

by our peace process correspondent, Dale Sunning

The SDLP has threatened to go into opposition if the rules are changed to prevent it going into government.

"The agreement was agreed by everyone so if everyone agrees to a new agreement then we won't agree to it," said party leader Mark Durkan.

"We will not be excluded, and we will exclude ourselves to prove it."

Titanic Struggle

by our transport correspondent, Dr Rhodes Hogg

TECHNICIANS in Belfast are working around the clock to free 1,700,000 people stuck on the same boat.

"The bow door remains jammed," said a spokesman yesterday. "Stern measures may be called for."

Bold arsonists?

by our crime correspondent, Rob Berry

Belfast fire chiefs say they have **done** all they can to investigate last week's major blaze. "The chance of finding evidence is **low**," said a spokesman.

"**You** have to realise that forensics is an **art**."

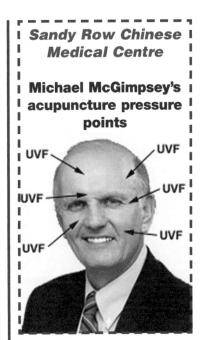
Gail Walker

Explaining global events with celebrity gossip

"So - Brian and Kerry McFadden's marriage has broken down. She wants a traditional home life but can also be bad-tempered and self-obsessed. He is more concerned with fame than family and has a weakness for cheap sex.

Which, if you think about it, is just like the relationship between Islam and the West."

Next week: If Darius can get a record deal then Kim Jong-Il can get plutonium.

Significant moves hope

by our peace process correspondent, Dale Sunning

Loyalists will make a significant move if republicans make a significant move, said loyalist sources yesterday. Republicans will make a significant move if the DUP makes a significant move, said republican sources yesterday. The DUP will make a significant move if Sinn Fein makes a significant move, said DUP sources yesterday. Sinn Fein will make a significant move if loyalists make a significant move, said Sinn Fein sources yesterday.

Get a move on, said everyone else yesterday.

B·B·C RADIO BLUSTER

Seamus Austin talks to South Belfast UUP councillor Michael McGimpsey.

Followed by Sectarian Thought for the Day

Seamus: Loyalists are organising racist attacks in your constituency.

Michael: I have no knowledge of that.

Seamus: Won't turning a blind eye to this disgust most UUP voters?

Michael: I have no knowledge of that either.

IRA in surface-to-air missile sales shock

SAMs your man for a bargain!

SORRY LITTLE EXCUSE

by our republican correspondent, Anne Phoblacht

BRIGHTON BOMBER Patrick Magee has offered his "sincere forgiveness" to victims of the 1984 attack.

Mr Magee's historic remarks can be heard on tonight's moving BBC documentary 'The Irish Freedom Fighter Who Nearly Killed That Bitch Thatcher'. *(Repeat. Not Ulster.)*

Camp followers shock

by our peace process correspondent, Dale Sunning

A man standing outside a tent pissing in has been asked to stand inside the tent and piss out.

"We believe the smell of piss will now go away," said an occupant of the tent yesterday, "or at least fade to a level we can learn to ignore."

Preparations have already begun to drain as much of the piss out of the tent as possible. "We'll never get rid of it all," admitted another occupant, "but they say this new guy can do excellent work on the ground-sheet."

Mind the shoes

Johnny Adair in 'gay picture' shock

Is this what they meant by 'Out before Christmas'?

Resistance fades

by our loyalist correspondent, Billy Shootspatrick

The DUP will engage with loyalists if it helps the peace process, said Peter Robinson yesterday.

"This is a significant change in party policy," explained Mr Robinson. "Until now we have only engaged with loyalists to undermine the peace process."

Memory problems?

by our republican correspondent, Anne Phoblacht

SINN FEIN has unveiled proposals for a 'Day of Reflection' on December 10th to remember all those who have died as a result of war and conflict.

The remaining 364 days of the year will be reserved exclusively for the remembrance of Pat Finucane.

The Portadown News

15TH NOVEMBER 2004   www.PortadownNews.com

RACIST ATTACK WHITEWASH

by our peace process correspondent, Dale Sunning

VIOLENCE against immigrants is much worse than violence against working-class white people, a North Down dinner party guest has confirmed.

"Something must be done about these terrible racist attacks," said NIO civil servant and lay magistrate Mrs Barbara Menary between mouthfuls of lobster yesterday. "However nothing must be done about attacks on everyone else, because that might destabilise the peace process."

BBC northern ireland

Derry City Beat
Follow the Foyleside plods on their 30-year journey from Bloody Sunday to another Bloody Saturday Night.

Swiss Bank Account Family Robinson
Washed up in County Down, can the Robinson family find shelter with just £250,000 in expenses?

Starring Jeffrey Donaldson as Man Good Friday

Century Farm   BBC Northern Ireland

This week: John is alarmed to learn that Japan has invaded Russia, Conor voices support for Theodore Roosevelt in the US presidential election, Fionnola welcomes the invention of the rectifying diode, and Marie celebrates the birth of famous novelist Graham Greene, starting a causality paradox that threatens to unravel the fabric of space-time.

Derry police test new CS gas spray

POLICE SERVICE of NORTHERN IRELAND
A Service to be Proud of

MIGRANT WORKERS - POLICE ADVISORY

What to do if you are attacked by loyalists:

1. Lie down

2. Close your eyes

3. Wait for the emergence of a disciplined political movement from within the loyalist community willing to engage in constructive dialogue with other parties in pursuit of an overall settlement

---

THE ROYAL BRITISH LEGION

With thanks

* * *

This year's annual row over poppies has been kindly sponsored, once again, by -

the IRISH NEWS

UTV

The Belfast Telegraph

Sinn Féin

News Letter
The pride of Northern Ireland

UDA proposal 'flawed'

by our loyalist correspondent, Billy Shootspatrick

UNIONISTS have criticised government plans to give the UDA £3 million to set up private security firms.

"We have no problem doing business with loyalists, as anyone on the ground in Larne, Lisburn, Ballymena, Coleraine, Bangor, Carrickfergus or Rathcoole can confirm," said a DUP source yesterday. "But if the UDA goes legit, nobody will need to hire private security firms."

The Portadown News

22ND NOVEMBER 2004   www.PortadownNews.com

UDA accepts NIO ceasefire

by our peace process correspondent, Dale Sunning

THE UDA has courageously agreed to recognise the Northern Ireland Office ceasefire. The NIO has promised a complete cessation of policing operations although it will retain the structures and appearance of a government organisation.

"Under the right circumstances I am also prepared to stand down," added secretary of state Paul Murphy yesterday.

"In fact under most circumstances I am prepared to lie down, roll over and let Andre Shoukri tickle my tummy."

Internal Housekeeping

This month: Paul Murphy shows us around his lovely ceasefire

Also: Curtains for the rest of you

Councillor Joe O'Donnell's retirement disco

Please do not request any house

Weird Tele billboard campaign makes no sense, asparagus

CHARITIES WARNING

by our republican correspondent, Anne Phoblacht

Paramilitary groups are using charities as a front for money laundering, claims a new report from the International Monitoring Commission. Suspect organisations include:

- The Nationalist Trust
- Greenpeaceprocess
- Trocaire Ar La
- Heartless Stroke Foundation

SDLP breaks ceasefire

by our security correspondent, Roger Base

SDLP councillor Danny O'Connor has fired a gun over the heads of a loyalist gang attacking his house. The incident has been condemned by Sinn Fein.

"This is absolutely typical of the stoops," said a republican source yesterday. "They couldn't hit a barn door."

Fare enough

by our transport correspondent, Dr Rhodes Hogg

TAXI drivers in Belfast have protested over a new government safety campaign which portrays them as thieves, drunks and rapists.

"This advertisement is grossly unfair," said a spokesman yesterday.

"Only the black-taxi drivers are thieves, drunks and rapists."

Folks on the hill

by our environment correspondent, Aaron Sweater

DIVIS Mountain will soon be open to the public thanks to its acquisition by the National Trust.

"We're expecting a huge response from the public," said spokesman Rusty Castle yesterday. "Belfast people like nothing better than a summit free-for-all."

Independent decommissioning witnesses agreed

→ DEADLOCK ←

DEADLINE ←

Too obvious?

by Linda, Jane

NEWTOWNARDS has been sealed off due to a large escape of harmless gas.

A spokesman for Downtown Radio was unavailable for comment.

GAA violence 'disproportionately affects Catholics'

See page 92

University area challenge

by our education correspondent, Una O'Level

THE peace process reached its logical conclusion last night when hundreds of students rioted in South Belfast, claiming that they had been discriminated against by the BBC.

"This is our area," said spokesman Grant Dole.

"We have been planted here by Queens against the wishes of the original inhabitants and are now in a majority, so we can do whatever we like."

The students dispersed after an appeal by Alex Maskey, because they were all fenians.

Birmingham bombing - public apology

"This was regrettable and should not have happened."

Birmingham apology - private explanation

This was regrettable as indeed were all deaths due to the conflict on both sides including a third side comprising English people sitting in pubs, although it was no more regrettable than other deaths on either side including a fourth side comprising Irish people blowing up pubs, because there can be no hierarchy of victims in the Ireland of Equals or for that matter in the England of Pubs. Unionists should not have created the causes of the conflict which caused the bombings to happen, so the bombings should not have happened. Hope that clears things up.

Yours in struggle
G. ADAMS

Identity cards 'will combat terrorism'

Political progress continues

The Portadown News

29TH NOVEMBER 2004 — www.PortadownNews.com

Make it go away

by our North West correspondent, Dermot Londondermot

THE Bloody Sunday Inquiry has concluded at a final cost of £155 million. Lord Saville is expected to rule that next time around it would be cheaper if the army shot 27 solicitors. The Pat Finucane Inquiry may disprove this finding.

ASSETS RECOVERY AGENCY

For public auction

Lot 1:
**Short political leash
NOT GOING!**

Lot 2:
**Any pretence that the law
applies to everyone
GOING!**

Lot 3:
**All police credibility
GONE!**

Happy bunnies - fluffy kittens

The soothing new political column, by Secretary of State Paul Murphy

JUST one week into the UDA ceasefire Northern Ireland is already a changed society. Businesses in North Belfast no longer pay protection money, Catholics ordered out of East Belfast have safely returned home, Rathcoole is as drug-free as a church picnic and any journalist who claims otherwise will be reported to their local brigadier. As Tony Blair said this week, "Terrorism is a very real threat to the United Kingdom, except in Northern Ireland where it is no threat at all..."

(continued until the next shooting)

(c) Northern Ireland Office

Craigavon Regional Area Plan

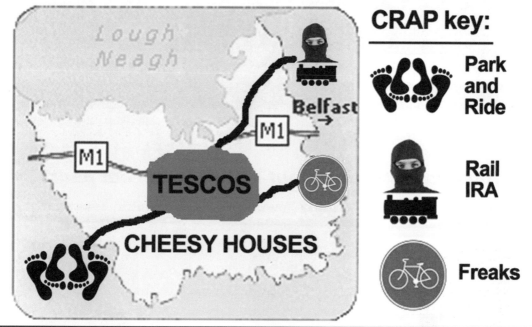

CRAP key:

Park and Ride

Rail IRA

Freaks

Last final closing endgame!

by our peace process correspondent, Dale Sunning

A **POLITICAL** deal looks tantalisingly close as speculation mounts that all sides are poised on the brink of a historic breakthrough and both governments urge further efforts while leading players declare it now or never with a deadline looming over strong indications of major movement on key matters despite considerable difficulties in certain areas under further discussion at top-level meetings where substantial progress on pivotal issues is now the focus of delicate talks on crucial concessions amid growing signs of renewed momentum...

...and so on

Blair feels "handover of history" on shoulder

... See page 98

The Portadown News

6TH DECEMBER 2004   www.PortadownNews.com

Have Your Say

How do YOU feel about a DUP-Sinn Fein pact?

Ian Gough-Barracks, Armagh	**Andy Townnews, Poleglass**	**Rabbi Tokenburger, Belfast**

"If Paisley say it's OK then it must be all right - and everything else he ever said must be all wrong."	"This historic chance for peace and unity must not be undermined by those dirty orange bastards."	"Why not ask me how I felt about the Nazi-Soviet pact."

Shame old story

by our republican correspondent, Anne Phoblacht

REPUBLICANS will not be humiliated, Gerry Adams told a cheering crowd of supporters in West Belfast yesterday.

The Sinn Fein leader then repeated his remarks in a language he clearly couldn't speak and unveiled a 30-foot-high mural of people smearing poo over themselves.

PORTADOWN NEWS INFOBOX

This week: a complete analysis of the factions behind the imminent UDA split.

1. Ecstasy dealers
2. Coke dealers

CEASEFIRE BROKEN

by our loyalist correspondent, Billy Shootspatrick

A FIVE-MAN gang has appeared in court charged with breaking the UDA ceasefire.

The suspects, all police officers, were accused of interfering with a bank robbery and behaviour likely to lead to a breach of the peace process.

They have been detained under the Prevention of Preventing Terrorism Act.

Bush in Paisley phone call shock

Are we talking about the same Camp David?

Progress on equality - everyone equally fed up

... See page 92

Contagion spreading

by our property correspondent, Des Res

THE infestation of woodworm at Ian Paisley's Martyrs Memorial church has spread to Gerry Adams' Donegal holiday cottage, it has emerged.

Sources are blaming an infected bodhran, or possibly a rifle butt.

"This was not unexpected," said one expert yesterday.

"It's a plague on both their houses."

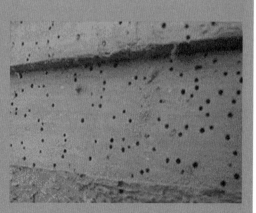

Another useless plank yesterday

CONTRAST RUINS BIG PICTURE

by our peace process correspondent, Dale Sunning

SINN FEIN will not provide photographs of decommissioning, it has developed.

Republicans are concerned about negative exposure while unionists want everything in the frame. With a snap decision unlikely and views becoming polarised, Tony Blair has urged both sides to focus. However Ian Paisley has retreated to a dark room while Gerry Adams says he may order blow-ups.

"The camera never lies," explained a Sinn Fein spokesman yesterday. "That's why we don't have one."

Northern Ireland Photography Tips

1. Check shutter

2. Select shot

3. Remove cap

Sammy Wilson demands humiliating photographs

...See page 98

PORTADOWN NEWS INFOBOX

Minimum requirements for filmed decommissioning

1. £600,000 Arts Council grant
2. Cameo appearance by James Nesbitt
3. Crown Bar snug scene
4. Juliette Turner soundtrack
5. No audience

Paisley considers further gestures

Embarrassing pictures: a guide

Would embarrass the IRA

Didn't embarrass the IRA

Text only

by our republican correspondent, Anne Phoblacht

THE IRA may consider something in the context of everything, security sources have revealed. This could involve one thing with the subtext of another thing or nothing on the pretext of anything. Tony Blair has hailed the move as "histrionic".

The Portadown News

20TH DECEMBER 2004   www.PortadownNews.com

Weapons crisis resolved!

by our peace process correspondent, Dale Sunning

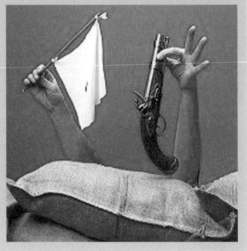

SINN FEIN has offered the DUP a solution to the weapons impasse which will satisfy both sides, it has emerged.

Under the deal decommissioning would be photographed by An Phoblacht for an exhibition at the West Belfast Festival, which would then go on permanent display at Conway Mill.

"This will provide a verifiable and transparent record of decommissioning," explained a republican spokesman yesterday. "However, no Protestant will ever get to see it."

Awful house seized

by our crime correspondent, Rob Berry

ANOTHER five-bedroom mock-Georgian house has been seized by the Tasteless Recovery Agency. Among the criminal wastes of money under investigation are a white uPVC conservatory, his'n'hers matching BMWs and a games room over the garage. Detectives also closed a stable door after the horse had bolted.

Library closures 'long overdue'

...See page 98

NORSEMEN BUY NORTHERN

by our business correspondent, Reg Empty

DENMARK's largest financial group has bought the Northern Bank.

"A thousand years ago we Danes came to your shores seeking only to loot and plunder, carrying off all your gold and leaving you destitute and homeless," explained a spokesman yesterday.

"By acquiring the Northern Bank, we will be able to pick up more or less exactly where we left off."

Liam Neeson in Paisley movie shock

Christ, not another Phantom Menace

The Portadown News

27TH DECEMBER 2004   www.PortadownNews.com

Sound of tree falling in forest 'must be recorded'

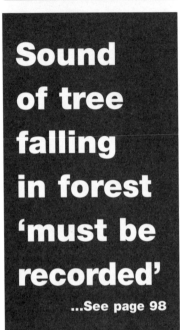

...See page 98

Humiliating Photographs: Part II

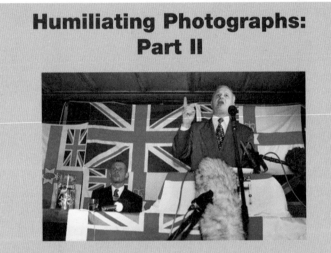

Willie McCrea shares a platform with Billy Wright at a 1996 LVF rally in Portadown, just two months after the LVF murder of Lurgan taxi driver Michael McGoldrick.

We don't take those mate

by our finance correspondent, Penny Wise

AN ENGLISH barman has refused to accept two million Northern Bank tenners, it has emerged.

"If it ain't got the Queen's head on it then I ain't takin' it," said the barman yesterday. "Yeah I know it says 'Belfast' on the front but that's in Ireland, innit?"

"Whaddya mean 'Ulster is British'?" added the barman. "I thought you said you was in the IRA."

Local family in lower middle class shock

PORTADOWN NEWS INFOBOX

How burning down a DIY store will unite Ireland

1. Unionists forced into power-tool sharing
2. Governments unable to shelve proposals
3. No more plastering over the cracks

Bank haul 'worth more than Catriona Ruane's Air Miles'

...see page 98

IMPORTANT CLARIFICATION

THERE is no link between this week's bank robbery and the IRA, senior Sinn Fein sources have claimed. There is also no link between Sinn Fein and the IRA, senior Sinn Fein sources have claimed.

Republican Raffles?

by our crime correspondent, Rob Berry

THE Northern Bank raid was "the work of criminal masterminds", say police sources.

"We are amazed by the careful planning, detailed logistics and professional execution of this ingenious crime," PSNI officer Bill Mason told reporters yesterday.

"The gang pointed guns at two unarmed people, drove them to Belfast, then told them to carry a load of useless Northern Ireland monopoly money out to a van. Clearly everyone involved has an IQ of at least 160."

Detectives say loyalist involvement has now been ruled out.

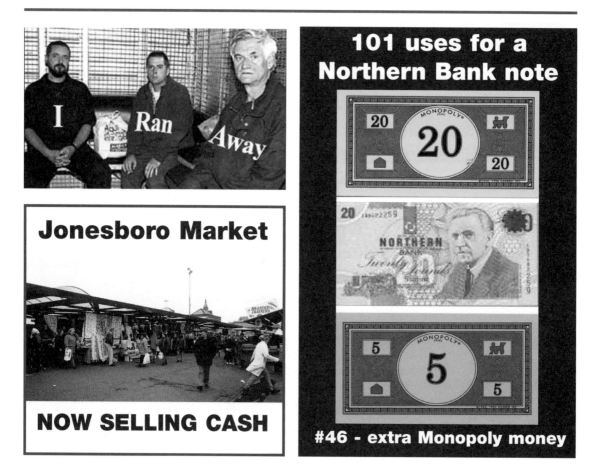

I Ran Away

Jonesboro Market

NOW SELLING CASH

101 uses for a Northern Bank note

#46 - extra Monopoly money

SECOND-CLASS VICTIMS

by our republican correspondent,
Anne Phoblacht

AN ENORMOUS wave of resentment has struck Sinn Fein as the world turns its attention to a genuine crisis.

"For the next week or so I suppose our thoughts should be with the people of South East Asia," said a party spokesman yesterday. "But as the initial disaster fades from the headlines, our long-term priority must be to remind the international community that the PSNI opened Eddie Copeland's Christmas presents."

A United Nations spokesman was too busy to comment.

ARDOYNE PUBLIC RELATIONS DISASTER APPEAL

Please help an innocent family who lost everything under their tree after police flooded the area. All donations will be compulsory, as usual.

Toys urgently required:

- Power-Sharing Rangers
- Barbie Brown (no Ken necessary)
- Thomas the Anti-Tank Engine
- 'Operation'

£22m

£0

The Portadown News

3RD JANUARY 2005   www.PortadownNews.com

Securocrat conspiracy fails to stop securocrat conspiracy

by our security correspondent, Roger Base

GERRY ADAMS has complained to Downing Street after a securocrat conspiracy to get Sinn Fein into trouble was not prevented by the much larger securocrat conspiracy to keep Sinn Fein out of trouble.

"Pointing out that we are undermining the peace process is undermining the peace process," warned a party spokesman yesterday. "Republicans are not criminals - you can bank on it."

PORTADOWN NEWS INFOBOX

A few other things the IRA has categorically denied

- Bombing Birmingham
- Bombing Claudy
- Bombing Enniskillen
- 'Disappearing' people
- Targeting civilians
- Florida gun-running

- Selling drugs
- Shooting drug dealers
- Killing Garda McCabe
- Knowing the Colombia 3
- Abducting Bobby Tohill
- Robbing Makro

...etc.

Wind causes power failure

... See page 98

Mad Dog an Englishman?

by our loyalist correspondent, Billy Shootspatrick

JOHNNY ADAIR may be flown directly to England on his release from prison to prevent a breach of the UDA ceasefire, security sources have confirmed.

"The UDA leadership has promised to kill Mad Dog if he stays in Ulster," said one source yesterday. "This leaves the government with no other choice, except keeping him in jail for the rest of his sentence, recognising the death threat as a ceasefire breach in itself, arresting the well-known UDA figures behind it and putting them behind bars as well. But that's just crazy talk."

STUPID SOW-AND-SOWS

by our environment correspondent, C. O'Twomey

THE bird sanctuary accidentally ploughed over at Strangford Lough may take years to recover, environmentalists have warned.

"Most of the worms have been cut in two by the plough," explained an expert yesterday. "After a sudden split they don't always know whether to grow a new head or a new arse."

The UDA was unavailable for comment.

HUGH'S HUGE HUSH

by our policing correspondent, Roz Peeler

PSNI Chief Constable Hugh Orde has held a three-week silence in memory of those who lost their credibility during the Northern Bank disaster.

During his lengthy period of reflection the Chief Constable prayed for all the many careers washed up in the tragedy, especially those found hanging from broken special branches.

The Portadown News

10TH JANUARY 2005   www.PortadownNews.com

Useless bankers

by our finance correspondent, Penny Wise

THE Northern Bank says it is still considering whether saying it is still considering withdrawing its current notes will make the robbers consider dumping the notes thereby removing the need to withdraw the notes - or whether saying it is still considering withdrawing the notes is not having the considered effect and considerable numbers of notes may actually have to be withdrawn. There was a charge of £20 for reading this article.

Loyalist mattress raided

by our finance correspondent, Penny Wise

SHOPS across Portadown report widespread panic buying as everyone sitting on a pile of dodgy cash rushes to spend it ahead of the Northern Bank note recall.

Among the items in demand are leather sofas, flatscreen TVs, gold jewellery, home gym equipment, holidays in Spain, Rangers season tickets and high-quality Dutch gay porn - however smaller businesses are also feeling the strain.

"If one more person tries to buy a Chunky Kit-Kat with a £100 note I'm closing early," warned a local newsagent yesterday.

Crying Butcher Game

by our peace process correspondent, Dale Sunning

ALL NEW development must stop until Northern Ireland finds a way to deal with its crap, planners have been warned. Meanwhile a ferry has run aground in stormy waters and a woman has had her legs cut off after being left out in the cold.

"We haven't seen this many naff peace process metaphors all at once since the last Neil Jordan film," said an Arts Council spokesman yesterday.

Another ship of fools

Sinn Fein demands rejection of 'rejectionist demands'

... See page 98

EXCLUSIVE!

Martin McGuinness talks to the IRA - only in the Mirror.co.uk

...see page 98

The biggest theft of waste paper in history

Peace process in our time...

Irish signs go metric

NOT A CENTIMETRE

Ulster experience benefits army

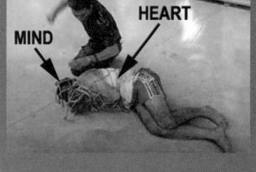

THE PORTADOWN NEWS PRESENTS:
Elements in the media

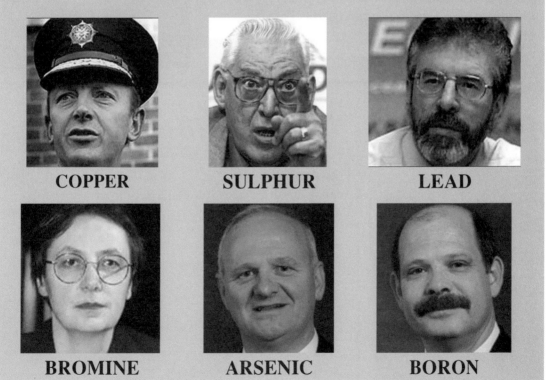

COPPER   SULPHUR   LEAD

BROMINE   ARSENIC   BORON

The Portadown News

24TH JANUARY 2005 — www.PortadownNews.com

Face responsibility

by our crime correspondent, Rob Berry

PUNCHING Mitchel McLaughlin in the face would be wrong but cannot be viewed as a crime within the context of a conflict situation, it has emerged.

"Of course I would like to see a set of circumstances which would bring about the removal of the causes of wanting to punch me in the face," said Mr McLaughlin yesterday.

"However what all of us on this island – and not just Sinn Fein – must recognise is that a considerable amount of work remains to be done to deliver that objective."

3,000 people were unavailable for comment.

Northern Ireland CRIMESTOPPERS
0800 555 111

I'm the sole rightful inheritor of the first Dail

How humiliating

by our peace process correspondent, Dale Sunning

REPUBLICANS have demanded proof of IRA involvement in the Northern Bank robbery.

"The government's word is not enough," said a Sinn Fein spokesman yesterday. "We need to see the evidence for ourselves."

Meanwhile unionists have accepted IRA involvement in the Northern Bank robbery.

"The government's word is enough," said a DUP spokesman yesterday. "We don't need to see the evidence for ourselves."

For technical reasons, this story could not be accompanied by a photograph.

COUNTER INSURGENCY

by our finance correspondent, Penny Wise

OVER 40 Northern Bank employees are to be moved to other jobs as a security precaution, the company has revealed.

"We hope to accomplish this as quickly as possible," said a spokesman yesterday.

"We just need a month to identify their national insurance numbers, then another three months to reprint their contracts."

Ich habe eine mandate!

BRIEF ENCOUNTER

by our legal correspondent, Daphne Diplock

NORTHERN IRELAND's top human rights lawyers have decided not to help the Guantanamo Four, the Portadown News has learned.

"Obviously we were interested in this case as it involves the British government," said a spokesman yesterday. "However we have had to turn it down as it looks like the men may be genuinely innocent."

The Portadown News

31ST JANUARY 2005   www.PortadownNews.com

TRAGIC ROUNDABOUT

by our children's television correspondent, Jack O'Nory

THE BBC has apologised to a Scottish sociology professor for employing a Protestant.

"It is true that Protestants are found in all nine counties of Ulster, but within Northern Ireland they are widely associated with sectarianism," wrote the professor during a brief lull in his hectic schedule. "I also find the term 'Blue Peter' to be offensively pro-Conservative."

The professor was watching children's television for research into his latest paper: Here's One I Made Earlier - Media, Symbolism and Imperialist Indoctrination (ages 5-14).

800,000 people who complained about 'Jerry Springer, The Musical' were not considered worthy of comment.

What? No hot-tub?

by our peace process correspondent, Dale Sunning

THE WORLD'S largest conservatory has been added to Stormont in a bid to tempt leading UDA figures into the peace process.

Sources say the project cost roughly £70 million but could not be more exact due to construction ambiguity.

The Ulster Political Voice Committee, which has an insight into itself, has given the news a cautious welcome. "It'll be great for all our plants, but there may need to be less transparency," warned a UPVC spokesman yesterday.

It's an injustice!

An occasional look at a topical issue through the grubby lens of paranoid tribalism

How Protestants get a raw deal on child abuse

PROTESTANTS

CATHOLICS

Abused by posh Belfast school:
£5,000/term

Abused by drunk Derry priest:
FREE

Fenian

Hun

Polarised Bears

Who's a pretty bhoy then?

Parrot of esteem

Guns under table taken off table over timetable

... See page 98

You *can* kill a burglar

by our crime correspondent, Rob Berry

BURGLARS can be killed in self-defence, the Home Office has announced.

"If a burglar enters your property our usual advice is to hide under the bed and hope that he goes away after pocketing as much as he can," explained a government spokesman yesterday.

"However if the burglar refuses to leave, physically prevents you from calling the police, repeatedly threatens your family, demands that you hand over everything including your bank details and keeps shouting 'I've got a gun!' whenever you try to reason with him well then, frankly, you've got every right to plug the bastard."

The Bridges of McAleese County

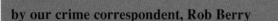

Arch stonewalling   Long suspension   Foyled (again)

Raid ruffles feathers

by our crime correspondent, Rob Berry

POLICE searching a Tyrone duck pond for evidence from the Northern Bank robbery have fractured a water main, it has emerged.

"We came under pressure to look for bills," explained a PSNI spokesman yesterday.

LOYALIST FEUD LATEST:
Who's running North Belfast?

JACKIE MAHOOD

Runs taxis

JANDRE SHOUKRI

Runs drugs

BILLY HUTCHINSON

Runs marathons

HUGH ORDE

Runs away

ROUTE OF ALL EVIL

by our transport correspondent, Dr Rhodes Hogg

IAN Paisley Junior has called for the immediate withdrawal of the new Translink Metro service.

"So-called 'Bendy Buses' were bad enough but painting them pink is the final insult," complained Mr Paisley yesterday. "I for one will not be getting on board the big pink bus no matter who thinks it might be my preferred mode of transport."

"The vast majority of people in Northern Ireland find 'Metrosexual' relationships offensive and obnoxious," added the DUP politician, "although I suppose an occasional double-decker is fair enough."

The Portadown News

14TH FEBRUARY 2005   www.PortadownNews.com

BUSH COMES TO SHOVE

by our American correspondent, Brad Cheesburger

DEMOCRATS will be punished for the failure of republicans if Northern Ireland's politicians are not admitted to the traditional White House St Patrick's day ceremony, David Trimble has warned.

Traditionally the St Patrick's Day ceremony punishes democrats and republicans in the White House for not admitting that Northern Ireland's politicians are failures.

Speaking to our reporter yesterday, a White House spokesman said, "David who?"

Prime Minister apologises for something he didn't do

Blind Mandate

SORRY

You had a great time, but...

YER HEID'S AWAE

by our Ulster-Scots correspondent, Rabbie Burns-Report

FORMER ULSTER-SCOTS boss Lord Laird was forced to travel everywhere by taxi due to security concerns, he has revealed.

"Clearly it would not have been safe for me to use the train, surrounded by dozens of other potentially-hostile first-class passengers; or the bus, where my kilt might have attracted the unwanted attention of little old ladies; or my own car, with its easily-identifiable 'W4NK3R' registration plates," said his Lairdship yesterday.

"That left me with no choice but to phone up complete strangers working for loyalist paramilitaries and give them directions to my house."

Illegal Orange parade 'just what the Short Strand needed' ... See page 98

The Portadown News

www.PortadownNews.com

Apology

The Portadown News wishes to apologise for any offence caused by our columnist Myra Jason in her recent article 'Scrounging slappers and their little bastards'. We did not realise that so many of our readers were single mothers, as we thought they only took their benefit money to the newsagents to buy fags and scratchcards. The editorial board of the Portadown News acknowledges that it was wrong to view the children of those readers as legitimate targets. Such children are, of course, illegitimate targets.

The rule of law for beginners

Shankill Road welcomes Mary McAleese

SINN FEIN BOMBS

by our security correspondent, Roger Base

SINN FEIN has been seriously injured by a massive no-warning implosion. Security sources believe the blast was caused by an improvised rhetorical device containing 26 million pounds of home-made bullshit.

At least 3,000 people are feared to be still dead.

"This implosion was a crime," said a Sinn Fein spokesman yesterday, "unless we triggered it ourselves, in which case it wasn't."

PORTADOWN NEWS INFOBOX

How the 12th of July 'festival' contributes £6 million a year to the local economy

■ Lost tourism	-£394,000,000
■ Police overtime	+£400,000,000
■ **TOTAL**	**+£6,000,000**

Notices

Question Time is coming to Belfast. If you would like to be in the audience please seek urgent medical attention.

As above.
Or kill yourself.

Trouble on the ground

by our housing correspondent, Des Res

UP to 1,700,000 people may have to leave their homes due to a contaminated land scare.

"The poison has seeped right down to the bedrock," warned a Housing Executive spokesman yesterday. "We've got no option but to clear everyone out, knock everything down and start all over again."

Relief from Derry

by our North West correspondent, Dermot Londondermot

PROTESTANTS across Northern Ireland breathed a huge sigh of relief after this week's sectarian attack on Linfield fans in Derry, it has emerged.

"Thank God," said one Protestant yesterday. "It's conclusive proof that Catholics are as bigoted as we are."

PORTADOWN NEWS INFOBOX

How the 'Obel Tower' will blend into Belfast

- Two lobbies
- Tall storeys
- Different views
- Pent-up-house

ANOTHER FINE MESS

by our republican correspondent, Anne Phoblacht

SINN FEIN has vowed to remain outside Stormont until it is paid to go away.

The republican family says it has nowhere else to go and is demanding a purpose-built halting facility.

"The British government has no right to tinker with us," said a spokesman yesterday.

"Building the peace process will require nerve and drive. Only Sinn Fein has the nerve to tarmac that drive."

Clark Gable

Letsnotbe Avenue

by our security correspondent, Roger Base

NEW house arrest powers will not be used against terror suspects in Northern Ireland, say government sources.

"The typical Northern Ireland terrorist owns so many houses that it's not worth the hassle," explained a spokesman yesterday.

The Portadown News

7TH MARCH 2005 www.PortadownNews.com

Policing breakthrough!

by our security correspondent, Roger Base

STOP PRESS: In a dramatic breakthrough for the peace process, Sinn Fein has asked to send representatives to the next meeting of every local policing board.

"This is a one-off exercise with several conditions but not pre-conditions attached," explained a party spokesman yesterday. "First, our representatives must be permitted to carry a large hold-all into each meeting which must not be searched. Second, upon arriving at the meeting they must be allowed to go to the bathroom by themselves, possibly for some time, depending on whether the walls are panelled or tiled. Finally, after returning from the bathroom they must be excused from the meeting to make an urgent phone call."

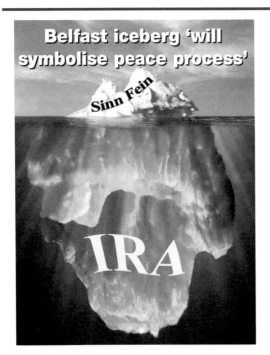

Belfast iceberg 'will symbolise peace process'

Sinn Fein

IRA

Adams responds to growing crisis

DUCK RESPONSIBILITY

by our republican correspondent, Anne Phoblacht

SINN FEIN is ill-prepared for an outbreak of bird flu, experts have warned.

The disease is spread by feather-bedding and the yolk of oppression, creating a deadly chicken and egg-type situation.

"If they don't take this seriously one of their wings will drop off," said a doctor yesterday. "They have no option but to isolate themselves from themselves and go completely cold turkey."

BBC spotlight

This week: Has money paid out by the Catholic church been paid into the church by Catholics?

Next week: Why hasn't the Catholic church paid out the money we stopped Catholics paying into the church?

...and so on

THIS SPORTING DEATH

by our peace process correspondent, Dale Sunning

DETAILS are emerging of the 'International Conflict Transformation Centre' to be built alongside Northern Ireland's new multi-purpose sports stadium.

The centre will feature exhibits covering 30 years of own-goals, amateur divisions, marked men, penalty shots, left-wingers, yellow cowards, drop-kicks, headers, fumbled tries, Jesus saves, offensive tackles, defensive dribbling, no-score draws, injury time, sudden death and balls.

"Our pitch is simple," said a spokesman yesterday. "We will show the world that Northern Ireland has its head up its astroturf."

HERE LIES A SOLDIER

by our republican correspondent, Anne Phoblacht

THAT IRA STATEMENT IN FULL:

Following an investigation of ourselves alone by ourselves alone several volunteers have volunteered to be shot.

This offer has been rejected.

Therefore we now order those we have expelled but who still remain under orders to appear in court where it can be assumed that their evidence will be ruled unsafe due to the threat we have not carried out but have made public, in the absence of any other evidence due to threats that the public can safely assume we will carry out.

May justice prevail.

P. O'Neill

 **NOTICE**

**Larne line closed
due to essential social engineering**

---

advertisement

Northern Ireland Tourist Board

Very short breaks

If you don't go, you'll never know!

JUDITH COLLINS

The column that holds nothing up

These media attacks on Sinn Fein are a disgrace. Have people forgotten about RUC collusion, loyalist death squads, decades of unionist misrule, the B-Specials and that time I didn't get a job at Queens because my eyes are too close together? Constantly casting back over the past 24 hours while ignoring the recent 800 years will not help us to move this process forward!

Judith's new book 'The Sorry Apologist' is out now.

Price: her soul.

Another stiff fine

by our crime correspondent, Rob Berry

POLICE have charged the Assets Recovery Agency with grave-robbing.

Officers discovered the public body digging up a private body after an LVF funeral.

"We cannot comment on a live investigation," said a PSNI spokesman yesterday.

This is believed to be the first time that the Assets Recovery Agency has been involved in a live investigation.

Radical 'Titanic Quarter' development plan unveiled

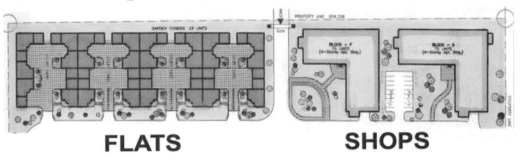

FLATS　　　　**SHOPS**

The Portadown News

21ST MARCH 2005   www.PortadownNews.com

Shinners talk balls

by our sports correspondent, George Worst

Sinn Fein has warned that a football is being used as a football.

"This is all part of a game," said a party spokesman yesterday. "By refusing to put the football in the locker the referee is deliberately taking us into injury time."

However the referee has denied the accusation. "I am as anxious as anyone to put this football away," he said. "However I can't do that until the whistle is blown."

Last night, in a completely unrelated development, Mitchel McLaughlin claimed that stealing whistles is not a crime "if the referee is a bastard".

SCORE SO FAR: 0-0

Horror at new Robert McCartney statement

McGuinness comments 'misinterpreted'

BBC RADIO BLUSTER

David Dunluce talks to the usual suspects.
Followed by Sectarian Thought for the Day

David: And on the line we've got Martin from Derry.

Martin: I support the family's search for justice - but who's funding this trip to Washington, eh? eh?

David: The American hosts, obviously. Danny from Poleglass, you've got a question?

Danny: I also support the family's search for justice - but who's funding this trip to Washington, eh? eh?

David: The American hosts, obviously. Gerry from Belfast, what are your thoughts?

Gerry: I too support the family's search for justice - but...

...and so on

New threat to McCartney women

Anyone need a lift?

The Portadown News

NOTICE TO READERS:

Our new compact morning edition does not replace the afternoon edition - at least not yet anyway.
Why not buy both so we can see how it goes before making our minds up?

Barmy council splits

by our unionist correspondent, Will March

The Orange Order has cut all ties to the Ulster Unionist Party. The historic decision was announced yesterday by Ulster Unionist MP the Reverend Martin Smyth (Grand Master, Orange Lodge of Ireland, 1972-96; Grand Master, Orange Lodge of World, 1974-82 and President 1985-88; Hon. Past Grand Master, Canada; and Hon. Deputy Grand Master, USA, New Zealand and Australia.)

"This is a bold step away from us by ourselves towards modernisation," said Party leader David Trimble (Grand Election Wizard, Drumcree, 1995-1996).

"If it doesn't prove that we're two separate organisations, I'll eat my bowler hat."

POOR WEE TIMMY!

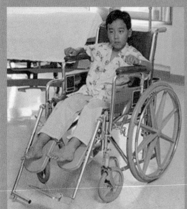

by every lazy reporter in Northern Ireland

SPECIAL needs pupil Timmy Token will DIE if Portadown Education and Library Board is forced to accept a massive 2% funding cut, a top civil servant warned yesterday by phone from the back of his chauffeur-driven Bentley.

"There will be further photogenic victims if the government doesn't drop its insane plans to abolish my job," added the civil servant while instructing his driver to take him home at lunchtime.

"Lollipop men will be run over, dinner ladies will starve and the P3 hamster will be drowned in a bucket at break-time. My secretary will fax you the details."

On other pages:
- **Timmy's slow death begins - full colour spread**
- **Education Board budgets - too boring to look into**

BBC northern ireland

FROZEN NORTH

100 BBC-NI employees find out what happens when a chill wind blows through the finance department

---

PORTADOWN NEWS POLL

Should Snow Patrol continue touring without Mark McClelland?

DUP SUPPORTERS

YES	NO	Isn't that devil music?

SINN FEIN SUPPORTERS

NO	YES	Aren't they all prods?

The Portadown News

NOTICE TO READERS:
The morning edition will be printed for a few more weeks for the sake of appearances.
Please never mention it again.

IRA makes new offer to McCartneys

Fancy going for a pint?

De Lorean Dies

LISBURN BEATEN UP

by our out-of-town correspondent, John Lewis

BELFAST is picking on Lisburn again, it has emerged.

Lisburn was walking to the shops and minding its own business when the older city tried to knock it down.

However Belfast has denied starting the fight.

"Lisburn is always hanging around the shops getting on like it owns them," said Belfast yesterday

"It thinks it's one of the big lads so it does but it's not so it isn't and I'll show it so I will."

Belfast also accused Lisburn of "slabbering", "showing off" and "stealing my Poleglass."

The Portadown News

4TH APRIL 2005   www.PortadownNews.com

Bent crust warning

by our earthquake correspondent, Mick Size

THE University of Ulster is about to be shaken to its very foundations, Indonesian scientists have warned.

Pressure is building along the Springvale Campus fault which last moved in 1998 causing £10 million to fall into a hole in the ground. Subsequent aftershocks also buried a report. This is putting additional strain on the rift between Jordanstown and Stormont, which already has enough on its plate.

Despite years of ominous rumblings many people in Northern Ireland remain unaware of

the large cracks opening up beneath the University of Ulster, as they are covered by a thick layer of management.

Sinn Fein debates election strategy

Tits support Northern Ireland

Burning indignation

by our crime correspondent, Rob Berry

YOUTH workers have blamed this week's fire at Portadown Community Centre on 'combustion in the presence of oxygen'.

"Obviously the fire was wrong, but the real problem is a lack of suitable facilities for exothermic chemical reactions," explained Youth Restorative Outreach Project Care Delivery Coordinator Mr Grant Dole yesterday.

"It's no wonder things ignite around here when so many vulnerable young oxidation processes have nothing else to do except hang around on the tips of matches and the ends of lighters."

Local residents described Mr Dole as "a flaming eejit."

Jim Gray in UDA expulsion shock

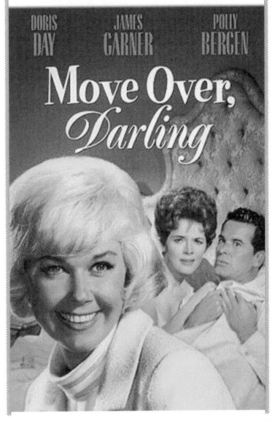

DORIS DAY   JAMES GARNER   POLLY BERGEN

Move Over, Darling

Holy unacceptable

by our religion correspondent, Helen Brimstone

A CATHOLIC priest has turned away two mismatched cousins, it has emerged.

The couple approached Father Mark Durkan and asked him to bless their union. However Father Durkan refused to officiate without his own family's permission.

"I told them to go and see Bishop Buckley," said Father Durkan yesterday. "He knows more about that sort of thing than I do."

The Portadown News

11TH APRIL 2005   www.PortadownNews.com

Paisley outlives Pope

by our religion correspondent, Helen Brimstone

MILLIONS of Catholics around the world are in mourning today as Ian Paisley remains very much alive.

Physicians attending the Free Presbyterian Pontiff say his heart and brain have stopped functioning but his spleen will last for decades.

Dr Paisley had been finding it difficult to talk but recently regained the ability before suddenly losing it again.

Meanwhile large crowds have gathered outside Castlereagh Town Hall, where white smoke has been seen coming out of Peter Robinson.

Female solidarity in Brussels

New secure unit for violent paranoid schizophrenics

Call centre boost for West Belfast

Can I interest you in protection payment?

MAN BITES EVERYONE

by our republican correspondent, Anne Phoblacht

GERRY Adams has called on himself to sit down.

"Sit! Sit! Sit Gerry!" said Mr Adams yesterday, adding "There's a good boy!"

Gerry Adams is standing for election.

Plank told to walk

by our peace process correspondent, Dale Sunning

FORMER Belfast Mayor Martin Morgan has opened the city's new Titanic Exhibition.

"When this great ship began to sink it is possible that some rats may have leapt overboard past the women and children," Mr Morgan told anyone still listening to him yesterday.

"But now that Belfast is bringing the Titanic back to life we should all recognise that rats are misunderstood little creatures with lovely fur and cute noses who deserve a second chance."

An SDLP spokesman offered to deck Mr Morgan immediately.

Near miss disaster

by our aviation correspondent, Avril Lancaster

DOZENS of children were not killed when a plane crashed into empty playing fields in East Belfast yesterday. Some of the children who were not killed could have had special needs, it has been speculated, while others might tragically have been close pals.

"Only the quick thinking of the pilot averted a much better story," thought every reporter in Northern Ireland. "Too bad he didn't crash into an off-licence and take out fifty of the little scumbags."

On other pages:
■ **Back to the bloody election**

East Belfast nose-dive 'could happen again'

I'll crash and burn!

Children punished

by our crime correspondent, Rob Berry

NORTHERN Ireland has been served with its first anti-social behaviour order. The troubled province, which is estranged from its parents and has a history of self-harm, has been ordered to stay at least 12 miles away from Scotland and refrain from using sectarian or made-up languages.

What's on your i-Pod?

DAVID TRIMBLE
'Split Wide Open'
 - Primal Scream

MARK DURKAN
'Vanishing Point'
 - New Order

GERRY ADAMS
'Peace Sells'
 - Megadeth

IAN PAISLEY
'Junior Painkiller'
 - Depeche Mode

because politics is an ugly business

Robbery crisis - police baffled

Didn't we tell the UDA to lay off for a while?

The Portadown News

18TH APRIL 2005   www.PortadownNews.com

New Pope is a Hun

by our religion correspondent,
Helen Brimstone

PROTESTANTS across Northern Ireland have been thrown into confusion by the appointment of a Bavarian pope.

In addition to being a hun, Pope Benedict XVI ran around with a right bunch of fascists in his late teens but bottled out of the army.

"It's like he's the anti-anti-Christ," said one perplexed loyalist yesterday.

"Well," added a DUP councillor, "I wasn't expecting the German Inquisition."

101 uses for a Northern Bank note

92. Quality control system

THERE IS A GOD

by our property correspondent,
Des Res

PORTADOWN estate agent John Philips has been remanded in custody on money laundering charges.

His tastefully-appointed accommodation comprises one reception-dining-bedroom-bathroom (2m x 1m) with off-white 'bucket-style' toilet, original feature window bars and panoramic exercise yard view. Bail was set at offers over £250,000 subject to court approval.

UUP election strategy at a glance

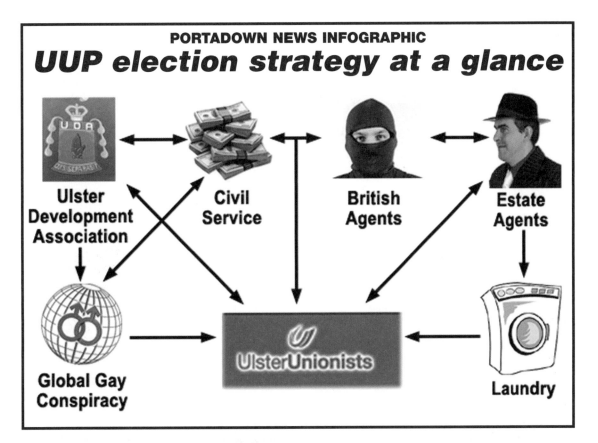

Ulster Development Association

Civil Service

British Agents

Estate Agents

Global Gay Conspiracy

Laundry

Decent People...

Leave Ulster

Vótáil Sinn Féin

Building Peace

Building Unity

Building luxury second homes in Donegal

NEAUX SURRENDER

by our unionism correspondent, Will March

The Ulster Unionist Party says it is disappointed that former leader Jim Molyneaux has endorsed rival DUP election candidates.

"As Ulster Unionists we are loyal to the Queen," said a party spokesman yesterday.

"If only the reverse was true."

Lollipop men face the axe

Sure you'll be grand

by our science correspondent, Bunsen Burns

AFTER two years of tests on 3,000 former patients, researchers at Lagan Valley hospital have proved that a few germs won't kill you.

The findings follow a breakthrough study on the effects of sticking a filthy endoscope down people's throats.

"We have finally established that your mother was right," confirmed a medical expert yesterday. "A bit of dirt never did anyone any harm."

Note: In light of this discovery, the Portadown News wishes to apologise for our November 2003 headline: 'Everyone in Lisburn has AIDS now'.

Inquiry latest: Victim still dead

See page 92

Oval vicious circle

by our sports correspondent, Ed Balls

THERE was more trouble in East Belfast this week when both sides got stuck into each other over some last-minute point scoring.

Police made several arrests as rival supporters hurled insults, accusations and writs.

"The other team only won by fielding our former players," said one angry UUP supporter yesterday.

"As far as we're concerned, that makes every goal an own-goal."

Final score: 0-0

NEIGHBOURS SAY FAMILY KEPT THEMSELVES TO THEMSELVES

by our consumer correspondent, Kaye Mart

ONE of Northern Ireland's best-known institutions is set to disappear, it has emerged.

'Sure It's Only a Few Eejits Ruining It for the Rest of Us' has been part of everyday life here for over 35 years, however from next week this much-loved staple will no longer be available.

Manufacturers D. Niall & Co. blame changing tastes for the decision. A new product, 'Sure Most People Don't Vote for Either of Them', will be on sale shortly.

Newsnight

Fresh from his ground-breaking interview with Martin McGuinness, Jeremy Paxman goes head-to-head with Pope Benedict XVI. Followed by bedtime.

Paxman: Your Holiness, do you wear a funny hat?

Pope: Yes, my son.

Paxman: Do you wear a funny hat?

Pope: I just told you…

Paxman: Do you wear a funny hat?

Pope: I'm wearing it right now.

Paxman: Do you wear a funny hat?

Pope: Everyone knows I do!

Paxman: DO YOU WEAR A FUNNY HAT?

…and so on

The Portadown News

2ND MAY 2005   www.PortadownNews.com

FIRST NORTHERN BANK PHOTO-FITS RELEASED

End of the line

by our transport correspondent, Dr Rhodes Hogg

PASSENGERS had a lucky escape yesterday when a train hit a car abandoned on the tracks outside Coleraine. The car was shunted very hard up the rear.

An NIR spokesman described the incident as "a sports massage".

X Rated

DUP
www.dup2win.com

Adams welcomes new Pope

UsterUnionists

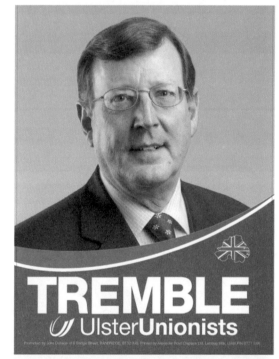

We've had our chips

TREMBLE
UlsterUnionists

ON OTHER PAGES:
Small election - nobody hurt

The Portadown News

9TH MAY 2005   www.PortadownNews.com

Hard to swallow

by our unionist correspondent, Will March

TANDRAGEE DUP assembly member Paul Berry has denied that a gay sex act took place between himself and a gay masseur he arranged to meet through a gay website.

"These allegations have come as a blow," admitted a party spokesman yesterday.

"However the DUP has worked long and hard to beat off the opposition and nobody will be pulling out at the last minute."

"We will continue to gobble up support," added the spokesman, "and we expect nothing less than a happy finish."

BROWN FINGER
The Portadown News gardening column

Dear Brown Finger
I wonder if you could settle an argument for me. Are berries a fruit?
Yours
Ian, Ballymena

Dear Ian
Yes they are - and they're delicious in a sticky jam.

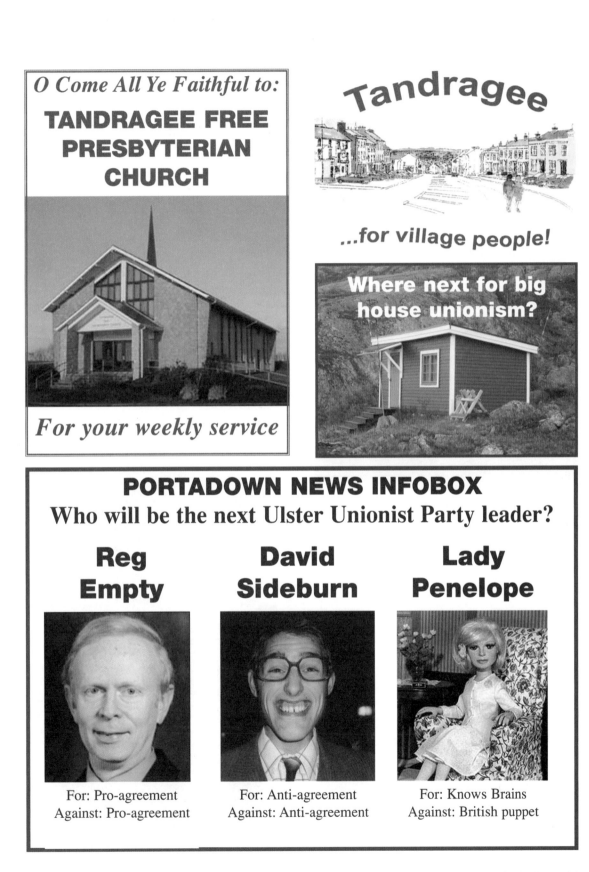

O Come All Ye Faithful to:

TANDRAGEE FREE PRESBYTERIAN CHURCH

For your weekly service

Tandragee

...for village people!

Where next for big house unionism?

PORTADOWN NEWS INFOBOX
Who will be the next Ulster Unionist Party leader?

Reg Empty

For: Pro-agreement
Against: Pro-agreement

David Sideburn

For: Anti-agreement
Against: Anti-agreement

Lady Penelope

For: Knows Brains
Against: British puppet

GONE TO GLORY

by every newspaper in the country

NORTHERN IRELAND has lost the greatest political leader that humanity has ever known. "David Trimble was a man of unprecedented courage, intelligence and modesty," said David Trimble yesterday. "Thanks entirely to his unique vision, Ulster Unionism is now respected around the world by all the people who have heard of it."

A former winner of the Nobel Peace Process Prize and Northern Ireland's first and last First Minister, Mr Trimble may now join the House of Lords, run the United Nations or become Emperor of Space.

BBC NEWSLINE
WEEKDAYS on BBC NI
1330, 1830 and 2230

Partina Murdy interviews DUP MP Nigel Dodds.

Followed by yet another adoption sob-story

Murdy: Do you still have confidence in your candidate?

Dodds: That matter is in the hands of our solicitors.

Murdy: Would those be skilled hands?

Dodds: That matter is in the hands of our solicitors.

Murdy: Will they put baby oil on their hands?

Dodds: That matter is in the hands of our solicitors.

...and so on

Final countdown

ALL the results are now in from the latest Northern Ireland Office survey (or 'election'). As always the Portadown News is first with a complete breakdown and analysis of the figures.

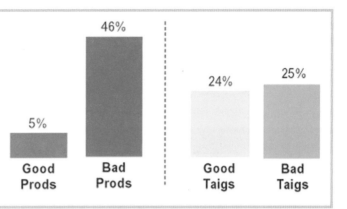

- 5% Good Prods
- 46% Bad Prods
- 24% Good Taigs
- 25% Bad Taigs

BBC WEATHER

BBC RADIO BLUSTER

David Dunluce talks to Newbuildings Community Centre spokesman Grant Dole. **Followed by despair.**

Dunluce: So is Newbuildings really the most sectarian place in Northern Ireland?

Dole: Certainly nat. Them fenians in Derry are much worse than we are so they are...

...and so on

Blacks and Tan

by our security correspondent, Roger Base

BACK yard oil tank fires may be the work of Al Qaeda, the new secretary of state has warned.

"Osama Bin Laden has ordered these attacks to push up oil prices and plunge the West into recession," explained Peter Hain yesterday. "That's why I support anti-terrorism legislation except in the case of the IRA, the UDA and the UVF."

"I was an anti-apartheid campaigner you know," added Mr Hain. "I'm much cooler than your dad."

The Portadown News

23RD MAY 2005   www.PortadownNews.com

Stringing us along

by our unionism correspondent,
Will March

CAPTAIN Scarlet has been replaced by the Mysterons, the Ulster Unionist Party has announced.

Three dead agents have been brought back to life under alien mind control to meddle in human affairs, for reasons that will never be properly explained.

"This is the voice of the Mysterons," said one.

"No, this is the voice of the Mysterons," said another. Meanwhile Lady Penelope has withdrawn from the leadership contest because she is only a Thunderbird. "Calling International Rescue, calling International Rescue" said a UUP spokesman yesterday.

New fire engines unveiled

Blair honours bomb squad

Ulster Young Militant no longer that young

by our loyalism correspondent, Billy Shootspatrick

LOCAL UYM leader Gary Linfield celebrates his 30th birthday today amid questions over his role in the youth organisation.

"I suppose some of the guys might think I'm a bit old but I don't expect anyone will make an issue out of it," said Gary. "Because if they do I'll kill them, like."

More money for Shorts

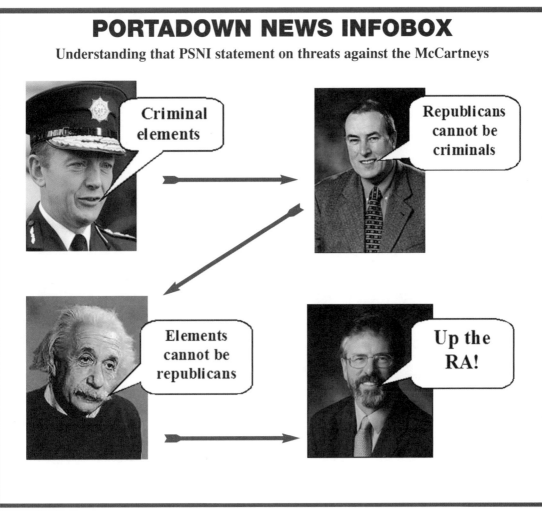

PORTADOWN NEWS INFOBOX

Understanding that PSNI statement on threats against the McCartneys

Criminal elements

Republicans cannot be criminals

Elements cannot be republicans

Up the RA!

GOING GOING GONE!

by our republican correspondent, Anne Phoblacht

FOLLOWING the successful auction of an MI5 bugging device, Sinn Fein has placed several more items of republican memorabilia on E-Bay. These include:

- One knife (cleaned)
- CCTV video tape (wiped)
- 4,000 bank bags (empty)
- 12 boiler suits (arse ripped out)

"We've already had a lot of interest," said a Sinn Fein spokesman yesterday. "5% APR on £26.5 million really stacks up."

Clinton remarks upset Paisley

Any chance of a sports massage?

David Simpson in Oliver Hardy shock

Spotter: J.K.

Lagan behind

by our Lisburn correspondent, John Lewis

A MAN has escaped from Lisburn, police have warned.

"I would advise the public to remain calm," said PSNI officer Bill Mason yesterday.

"It is very unusual for anyone to escape from Lisburn."

Special needy

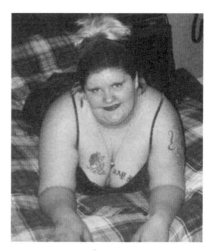

by our social affairs correspondent, Grant Dole

POPULAR local girl Shelley-Anne McAvoy has complained to the Equality Commission about media coverage of teenage mums.

"How come those three slappers in England got on the TV?", said Ms McAvoy yesterday. "I was 12 when I had our Tyler and I wasn't even in the paper. It's discrimination so it is."

Ardoyne Old Firm riot - police baffled

JUDITH COLLINS

The column that holds nothing up

After much soul-searching, our republican columnist feels it is time for an honest debate about the McCartney murder.

"What about Lisa Dorrian? What about Lisa Dorrian? What about Lisa Dorrian? What about Lisa Dorrian? What about Lisa Dorrian? What about Lisa Dorrian? What about Lisa Dorrian? What about Lisa Dorrian? What about Lisa Dorrian? What about Lisa Dorrian? What about Lisa Dorrian?..."

...and so on

Anthropomorphism

by our wildlife correspondent, David Rottenborough
A CUTE monkey story has escaped from Northern Ireland.

The cute monkey story got out on Monday and has since been spotted in the Daily Telegraph, the Guardian and Sky News.

"Looks like another teenager has had a row with his dad," said a lot of middle-aged male reporters wearily.

The Portadown News

6TH JUNE 2005   www.PortadownNews.com

"A NO BRAINER"

by our business correspondent, Reg Empty

NEW environment minister Lord Rooker has given the go-ahead to the controversial John Lewis department store scheme, which will simultaneously create and destroy 1,000 jobs by replacing Lisburn with a big shed.

"I am not an expert on planning or retailing," admitted Lord Rooker yesterday. "However I am also not elected or accountable so I can do any damn thing* I like."

"I've never felt so free, so alive," added Lord Rooker. "My God, the power! Muhahaha! MUHAHAHA!..." etc.

* Subject to an Equality Impact Assessment

Ireland - nul point

James Galway in Saddam Hussein shock

JOB SURVEY SHOCK

by our social affairs correspondent, Grant Dole

CATHOLIC women are over three times more likely to be unemployed than Protestant women, it has emerged.

This is entirely due to laziness.

The all-new iProd

Thanks to Neil Carey

New PSNI helicopter unveiled

The other foot

by our crime correspondent, Rob Berry

SINN FEIN has reacted angrily to police claims that the IRA was not involved in the Boots robbery.

"Where's the evidence?" said a party spokesman yesterday.

No third degree

by our education correspondent, Una O'Level

THE University of Northern Ireland (formerly Province Poly) has asked its Vice Chancellor to 'retire' on a pension equivalent to his full salary plus a lump sum plus profit sharing from numerous university companies.

"We were told to give him the sack," explained a spokesman yesterday. "We assumed that meant a sack full of cash."

The Portadown News

Tim not that dim

by our unionist correspondent, Will March

GULF war hero Colonel Tim Collins has ruled himself out of the Ulster Unionist Party leadership contest.

"I have no experience of politics or the issues affecting ordinary people," explained Colonel Collins yesterday.

"In fact I have spent my entire adult life telling working class men to stop thinking for themselves and obey my orders without question, because I went to grammar school and they didn't."

"See?" said John Taylor. "He's perfect."

Presbyterian Computers

- Drives removed

- Moderators Installed

MAKE HISTORY HISTORY

Daily Northern Ireland?

by our security correspondent, Roger Base

THE Assets Recovery Agency has announced a new strategy to bankrupt the UDA.

"We're going to ask them to launch a daily newspaper," explained a spokesman yesterday.

NESTS FEATHERED

by our ornithology correspondent, Robin Fowler

BBC Northern Ireland's 'Supergoose' programme has been reported to the Equality Commission, it has emerged. "All six participants are clearly republican," explained a spokesman yesterday. "They have two wings, some neck and expect the rest of us to watch them flapping about."

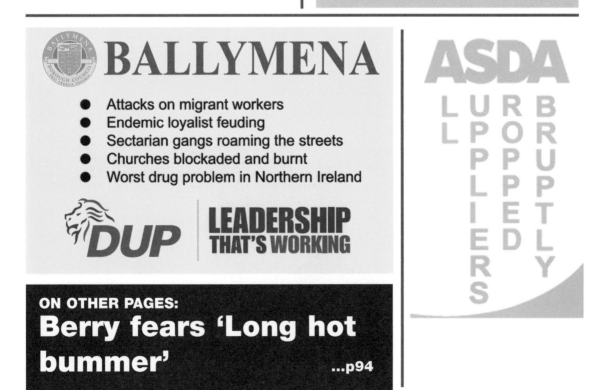

BALLYMENA

- Attacks on migrant workers
- Endemic loyalist feuding
- Sectarian gangs roaming the streets
- Churches blockaded and burnt
- Worst drug problem in Northern Ireland

DUP **LEADERSHIP THAT'S WORKING**

ASDA
LURB
LPORR
POPU
PPP
PLIEDT
ERS
DLY

ON OTHER PAGES:
Berry fears 'Long hot bummer'
...p94

Portadown News InfoBox

What would an IRA 'commemorative association' have to commemorate?

La Mon

Shankill

Warrington

Bloody Friday

Birmingham

Enniskillen

SNIPER AT WORK

Queen tells RIR she may visit republic

Lambeggars can't be choosers

by our unionist correspondent, Will March

UNIONISTS have warned that there will be rioting in East Belfast unless they are allowed to riot in East Belfast.

"The Parades Commission is asking for trouble by asking people to prevent trouble," said a DUP spokesman yesterday. "If Orangemen are held responsible for the behaviour of their hangers-on then they cannot be held responsible for the behaviour of their hangers-on."

Belgian waffle

by our republican correspondent, Anne Phoblacht

IRISH has been made an official working language of the EU.

"This is a great day for the Sinn Fein team at Brussels," said a party spokesman yesterday.

"Now Barbara de Bruin might actually do some work."

THE BILLY WRIGHT INQUIRY

Does it bother you that the government killed Billy Wright?

YES ☐

NO ☐

ONLY THAT IT TOOK THEM SO LONG ☑

Fears over clamping plan

The Portadown News

27TH JUNE 2005   www.PortadownNews.com

IRA debates new image

GRIM FAIRY TALES

Empty-Dempty sat on the fence

Waiting for his turn to commence

Until all the Queen's subjects

And all the Pope's flock

Got thoroughly sick of him

watching the clock

INTERFACE OF AN ANGEL

by our republican correspondent,
Anne Phoblacht

SINN FEIN fears that serious violence will erupt this summer if Northern Ireland's leading peace activist and cross-community negotiator, Sean Kelly, is not released from custody.

"Would it have killed them to give us some sort of warning?" asked a party spokesman yesterday. "We don't know who shopped him but the whole thing is very fishy."

"During the marching season a lot of people are on a very short fuse," added the spokesman. "That's when Sean always comes in handy."

EU defends cow subsidies

New IRA search for disappeared

Where's Sean?

 NORTHERN IRELAND
HUMAN RIGHTS
COMMISSION

Monica's draft Bill of Rights

1. **Everybody has the right to a £70,000 a year quango job if they can't get elected but still think they're pretty important.**

2. **Nobody has the right to complain about it.**

Potential difference

by our Foyle correspondent, Dermot Londondermot

THE DUP is demanding the immediate closure of Derry's new Coolkeeragh generating station, which will supply electricity to both sides of the border.

"This plant must be fully decommissioned before there can be any power-sharing," explained a party spokesman yesterday.

BBC website in Portadown News Shock

BBC NEWS UK EDITION — WATCH BBC NEWS IN VIDEO

News Front Page
World
UK
England
Northern Ireland
Scotland
Wales

Northern Ireland
Last Updated: Wednesday, 22 June, 2005, 17:04 GMT 18:04 UK

Ice cream man has assets frozen

A Belfast ice cream salesman has assets worth almost

OTHER TOP STORIES
- 'No review' of contested parade
- Man is jailed over video attack
- Wheel clamping plans announced
- Omagh bomb trial is delayed

SWINGING BOTH WAYS

by our unionism correspondent, Will March

SPECULATION is mounting over Paul Berry's position on Belfast's gay pride parade, which has been referred to the Parades Commission due to Christian objections.

"He'll want to support the religious protest but he'll also want to support the right to march," explained a DUP spokesman yesterday. "I suppose he could stand with the protestors for just long enough to keep them happy, then join the parade and bring up the rear."

"Poor lad," added the spokesman. "He must be terribly confused."

Smoking ban 'may be delayed'

Bee Specials in sting operation

Horror over brutal British oppression

by our republican correspondent, Anne Phoblacht

GERRY Adams has called for more government funding for the West Belfast Festival.

"It's disgraceful that no extra money can be found for this unique cultural event," said the millionaire President of Ireland's richest political party yesterday. "An extra £26.5 million, for example, would buy 52 million Frances Black albums from the garage with enough left over to give every member of Girls Aloud a decent Brazilian."

LONELY LOYALISTS

by our loyalism correspondent, Billy Shootspatrick

LOYALISTS in East Belfast have denied attacking a man's house because they thought his girlfriend was Catholic.

"We just attacked his house because he has a girlfriend," explained a loyalist source yesterday.

Sinn Fein calls for suicide strategy

belfast city council presents:

opera in the gardens

Swan Lake

The Magic Flute

Don Giovanni

Belfast solves St Pat's day problem

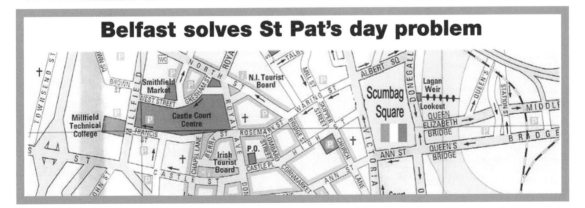

New loyalist feud fears

Goat beaten to death

Residents flee seeping poison

Bent-double standard

by our unionist correspondent, Will March

LISBURN has banned gay weddings in council offices.

"There can only be gay sex in council offices," confirmed a UUP spokesman yesterday.

Warning of threat 'not threatening'

by our republican correspondent, Anne Phoblacht

GERRY Adams has warned there will be violence at next week's Ardoyne parade if anyone mistakes his warning for a threat.

"Gerry is fed up with people treating his warnings as threats," warned a Sinn Fein spokesman yesterday.

"A warning and a threat are quite different. For example, only one needs to be accompanied by a recognised codeword."

NICE LITTLE ERNER

by our health correspondent, Florence Vulture

ENNISKILLEN's new Private Finance Initiative hospital will be built by Lakeland Meats, it has emerged.

The entirely Lithuanian-staffed facility will not provide emergency care, intensive care, specialist care or acute care but it will take full advantage of the region's "world-class diseased-carcass handling expertise", according to an NIO spokesman.

Meanwhile the Equality Commission has asked Lakeland Meats to expand its popular 'Soylent Green' range. 'Soylent Orange' will be in the shops shortly.

Portadown News Infobox

What Olympic events could be coming to Northern Ireland?

Poll Vault   **Long Jump**   **Shot Put**

Like old times

by our transport correspondent, Dr Rhodes Hogg

THE Railway Preservation Society of Northern Ireland has thanked republicans for this week's security alert on the line at Lurgan.

"Takes you back, doesn't it?" said a spokesman yesterday.

The Portadown News

18TH JULY 2005   www.PortadownNews.com

Balance restored to the universe

by our social affairs correspondent, Grant Dole

POLICE have praised republican protestors at this week's Ardoyne parade for proving that one lot is still as bad as the other.

"It was touch and go there for a while," said PSNI officer Bill Mason yesterday. "Right until the very last minute it looked like the Orange Order would end the day clearly in the wrong. But then 300 local scumbags turned up and normal ambiguity was quickly restored."

Trouble at gay pride parade

UNATTENDED BAGGAGE

by our security correspondent, Roger Base

LONDONERS have expressed their sympathy with the people of Northern Ireland following this week's terrible events.

"Everyone is very concerned," said one commuter yesterday.

"This morning on the tube I just couldn't stop worrying that the protest in Dunloy represents a clear escalation of nationalist demands."

Coastguard

Save

Only

Scots

Tim Glibney

The column that holds nothing up

IT is important to remember that the IRA never planted bombs in London with the deliberate intention of killing innocent people. When the IRA wanted to kill innocent people it planted bombs in Birmingham.

Huge crowds celebrate twelfth

DUP launches fruit juice

The Portadown News

25TH JULY 2005   www.PortadownNews.com

MAN BITES PUP

by our loyalist correspondent, Billy Shootspatrick

THE Progressive Unionist Party has accused the government of trying to push it out of politics. The Secretary of State has fined the PUP £25,000 for ongoing paramilitary activity - equivalent to half a kilo of cocaine, 500 Radio Ulster appearance fees or £12,500 per recent murder.

"This sort of repression is completely unnecessary," said a loyalist spokesman yesterday. "At this rate we'll all be dead by Christmas - and nobody votes for David Ervine anyway."

The Siege of Father Troy

Anger over Ryanair ad

LONDON FIGHTS BACK

Send the Micks to Stansted

Network Too

by our quango correspondent, Ernie Stacks

THE new head of the Equality Commission is former RTE boss Bob Collins, it has emerged.

"I'll fax you over the details in a minute," said an Equality Commission press officer yesterday. "But first you'll have to listen to some bells while looking at a picture of the Virgin Mary."

Saucy gander

by our unionist correspondent, Will March

THE DUP has warned that people could be injured if a republican parade takes place in Ballymena.

"This cynical attempt to expose our double standards will make people's heads spin, possibly causing them to fall over," said a party spokesman yesterday.

LEGAL AID

The new advice column with Jude Law

AS a legal expert I am often asked: "Can the police charge someone without a complaint?" The answer is no - indeed this has never happened once in the entire history of Northern Ireland.

For example, if you go up to a PSNI officer in the street and scream: "Why don't you useless bastards ever do your fucking job?" the officer will be powerless to act unless a passing member of the public adds: "Gosh, that was terribly rude."

LOYALIST CIRCLES

by our loyalist correspondent, **Billy Shootspatrick**

POLICE in East Belfast have refused to tackle a UVF mob which is tackling an LVF mob which police refused to tackle.

Residents had complained to police about the LVF mob before the arrival of the UVF mob but police say residents have not complained about the UVF mob.

"We just can't act unless we receive a complaint, unless it's about the LVF, in which case we can't act on just a complaint," confirmed PSNI officer Bill Mason yesterday.

ARDOYNE RIOT 12th JULY 2005
Can you identify these suspects?

Adams quits Army Council

They're worse than Lisburn Council

ON OTHER PAGES:
Small IRA statement - nobody hurt

Sean of the dead

by our republican correspondent, Anne Phoblacht

SHANKILL bomber Sean Kelly has been released a month after he was arrested for being "a danger to others".

"The timing of recent events indicates a well planned securocrat conspiracy," said a Sinn Fein spokesman yesterday.

"The leadership of this party will not rest until it has tracked down every one of those securocrats and thanked them in person."

Dangerous repairs attempted

Facelift for Ulster Museum

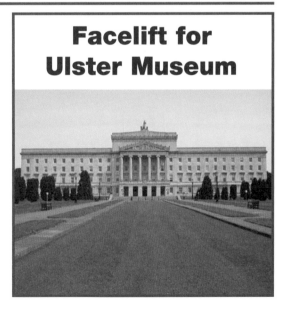

The Portadown News

8TH AUGUST 2005 — www.PortadownNews.com

Finding Neverland

by our unionist correspondent, Will March

IAN Paisley has vowed to keep Sinn Fein out of government by keeping himself out of government.

"There will be no surrender to the IRA's surrender," said the leader of Northern Ireland's largest party yesterday. "After fifty years in politics, republicans are still as dangerous as I have always needed them to be and it is still not my fault."

"It's true that we can't stop further concessions without a return to devolution," added Dr Paisley. "However we can stop a return to devolution. That'll show them!"

IRA statement

There will be a total cessation of everything we did during the last total cessation.

P. O.Neill

UUP BACKS ORLAITH

by our unionist correspondent, Will March

BIG Brother contestant Orlaith McAllister has won the backing of the UUP, it has emerged. "Orlaith is obviously a unionist," explained a party spokesman yesterday. "Gay people make her cry, she parades her tits all over the place and when she's losing she walks out."

Probe call

by our health correspondent,
Florence Vulture

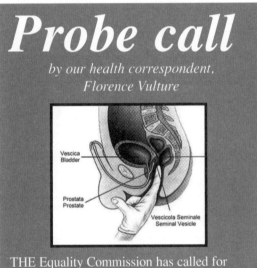

THE Equality Commission has called for Britain's bowel cancer screening programme to be extended to Northern Ireland.

"The government must pay us to look up our backsides," warned a spokesman yesterday

TIM GLIBNEY

The column that holds nothing up

THE end of the RIR is news that will be welcomed by all Irish republicans. It was nothing more than a sectarian militia, unlike the IRA which fought a noble and legitimate campaign against ... other protagonists to the conflict in which ... both sides suffered equally ... and we must all recognise ... nobody has a monopoly on ... there can be no hierarchy of ... there is a time for war and a time for ... everyone needs to recognise that ... the reality is ... the reality is ... aaaaarggh ... aaaaarggh ... AAAAAAARGGH!

Court crisis looms

by our security correspondent, Roger Base

CIVIL liberties groups have condemned the abolition of Diplock courts. "Juries will find people guilty," warned a human rights lawyer yesterday.

The Portadown News

15TH AUGUST 2005   www.PortadownNews.com

PSNI *on the blanket*

by our loyalist correspondent, Billy Shootspatrick

THE PSNI has issued fire blankets to Catholic residents in Ahoghill to prepare for imminent loyalist attacks.

Police also gave householders advice on personal security, escape routes, hiding under tables, packing in a hurry, applying for emergency accommodation and pretending to be Protestant.

Meanwhile, Catholic residents in Ahoghill have issued handcuffs to the PSNI. Householders also gave police advice on arrest procedures, relevant offences, hurrying up, not hiding under tables, applying themselves and not pretending they don't know the name and address of every loyalist in a ten-mile radius.

Rape case: Every little spide in Belfast wanted

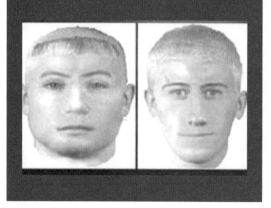

Colombia 3 break cover

Suspect device

by our security correspondent, *Roger Base*

THE army says a bomb abandoned in Lurgan this week had a sophisticated timing device.

"It was set to go off just after the IRA statement but just before people start asking why the IRA hasn't decommissioned yet," explained Lt. Col. Julian Sandhurst yesterday.

Nobody has been taken in by questioning.

Response to Channel 4's 'Location Location Location'

Strabane District Council rejects the claim that this is the third-worst town in the UK. Strabane has many attractions including a printing museum, statues on the bypass and prints of the statues on the bypass at the museum. Celebrities who have holidayed in Strabane include Tiger Woods, Mick Hucknall and Mick Hucknall's friends.

High unemployment figures are due to people from Lifford sneaking over the border to sign on and crime continues to fall now that everything not screwed down has been stolen.

Besides we're not in the UK, we're in Ireland. Up the 'RA!

Ballymena Showgrounds
presents

'Clash of the Culchies'

Introducing:

The INLA

Vs

Various Loyalists

* *Special appearance by the DUP*
** *Special disappearance by Sinn Fein*

Take her home?

by our republican correspondent, *Anne Phoblacht*

DESPITE their terrible ordeal the Colombia 3 don't find Catriona Ruane attractive, it has emerged.

"They've spent a year in the jungle, three years in prison and six months at sea - and they still wouldn't touch her with yours," confirmed a Sinn Fein spokesman yesterday.

Ms Ruane was unavailable for comment as the Colombia 3 have no knowledge of her whereabouts.

Caption Competition